THE ART CRISIS

Bonnie Burnham

THE ART CRISIS

St. Martin's Press New York

St. Martin's Press, Inc., 175 Fifth Avenue., New York, N.Y. 10010.
Manufactured in the United States of America
Library of Congress Catalog Card Number: 75-9469

Library of Congress Cataloging in Publication Data

Burnham, Bonnie.
The art crisis.

Includes bibliographical references and index.
1. Art—Marketing. 2. Art as an investment.
I. Title.
N8600.B87 338.4'7'7 75-9469

To my parents

CONTENTS

ACKNOWLEDGEMENTS

I owe my sincere thanks to a large number of people who have contributed to this book by giving interviews or discussing with me various aspects of the issues at hand. Among them, I would especially like to acknowledge my appreciation to several persons whom I have known professionally, and whose influence and importance might not be readily apparent to the reader.

My first debt is to Hugues de Varine-Bohan, former Director of the International Council of Museums. It is he who first introduced me to many of the problems discussed here, and who was the impetus behind ICOM's involvement with them. At ICOM he was both a guide and an enthusiastic collaborator, who willingly shared with me his vast knowledge of museum and cultural affairs, and who encouraged me to publish much of the information this book contains. Also at ICOM I should like to thank Dr Grace Morley, Director of the ICOM Regional Agency in Asia, and Ann Zelle, former Executive Secretary of US-ICOM, for their cooperation and frequent advice. I am greatly indebted to the staff of the UNESCO-ICOM Museum Documentation Centre, especially Mme Paulette Olcina and Mme Anne Raffin, for making valuable documentary material available to me. I am also grateful to Clemency Coggins, Porter

McCray, and Karl Meyer – all pioneers in exploring the antiquities crisis and searching for solutions to it.

During the writing of this book, I have greatly profited from conversations with Peter Hopkirk, who generously read and criticized the manuscript, Geraldine Norman and Richard Walter, who acquainted me with the London auction room and art market, and Dorothy Kraus, who made available information about misericordes. I am particularly grateful to Mr Norton Simon who generously agreed to talk to me about his purchase of the Sivapuram Nataraja, and to Miss Julia Mayer of the Norton Simon Foundation, for her help in correcting this chapter and bringing it up to date. Among the police specialists who co-operated by furnishing details and allowing me to publish certain information, I am especially grateful to Jacques-Paul Mathieu and Charles Pontramon of the Brigade Centrale de Répression des Vols in Paris, to Robert Volpe of the New York Art Squad, and Sid Wisker, formerly of Scotland Yard; to Kenneth Giannoules of Interpol in Washington, and to Robert Sauger and André Bossard of Interpol in Paris. I should also like to thank Turkish Airlines for providing an opportunity to visit the archaeological sites of Western Anatolia.

Finally, I owe many thanks to Hope Leresche, Jane Conway-Gordon and Philip Ziegler for their encouragement and support; and to Jack Flam, my deepest thanks for his invaluable help throughout the writing of the book.

For permission to quote from other works, I should like to thank Mr André Bossard of Interpol who has kindly allowed me to quote the letter reproduced in chapter 4; Professor Dwight B. Heath for permission to quote his article 'Economic Aspects of Commercial Archaeology in Costa Rica', and the English draft of his article 'En Busca de "El Dorado": Algunos Aspectos Sociologicos del Huaquerismo en Costa Rica'; and Gladys Davidson Weinberg, Assistant Director of the Museum of Art and Archaeology of the University of Missouri, for permission to quote her letter to ICOM on the ethics of acquisition. I am grateful to the publishers for permission to quote from Allen Wardell, 'Mayan Treasures at the Art Institute of Chicago' (*Apollo*); Clemency Coggins, 'Archaeology and the Art Market' (*Science*); Karen O. Bruhns, 'The Methods of Guaqueria; Illicit Tomb Looting in Colombia' (*Archaeology*); Calvin Tomkins, *Merchants and Masterpieces* (*Dutton*); Sotheby's *Belgravia* auction catalogue and yearbook *Art at Auction*; and *Christie's Review of the Year 1968–69*.

INTRODUCTION

Art, today, is news. Publicity for exhibitions and saleroom columns provide daily reading. New record prices are constantly being established for such diverse objects as Old Master paintings, African bronzes, and Chinese jars. Spectacular art thefts receive front page coverage, and scandals involving museum acquisitions have made us aware that the moral position of public institutions is not always above reproach. Yet we are seldom reminded that all these events are part of a larger problem, which touches everyone who collects, studies, or simply enjoys art. For as the art of the past has become increasingly popular and the prices of fine art objects have risen accordingly, a conflict has developed between the negotiable value of art and its spiritual function. And from this conflict phenomena have arisen which, taken together, constitute a real challenge to our ideas about art and culture.

The most obvious manifestation of this challenge is the way in which the art of the past has become victim to unprecedented pillage, theft, and destruction. Temples in obscure corners of the world are torn apart so that chunks of stone can be brought to museums in 'civilized' centres. Paintings and other artifacts are stolen from churches. An organized underground brings this loot to markets where buyers are willing to put aside their normal scruples; museums commission the pillage of archaeological sites, otherwise honest businessmen buy without hesitation objects that can only have been stolen, tourists become smugglers, and legitimate auctioneers party to fraud.

A related and equally alarming phenomenon is that, as the demand for fine art objects has risen, so the objects themselves have become paradoxically less accessible to the public at large. It might even be said that as the financial value of art objects has increased, their function as art has diminished. The same increased demand that has dictated higher market values and made art objects the prey of smugglers and thieves, has also put the possession of important objects beyond the reach of any but institutions and the most wealthy individuals. Institutions cannot solve the problems of increased crowds and unsatisfactory presentation, and the contemporary private collector is often more interested in the investment value of an object than in its value as art. Thus the art objects, so voraciously sought by museums and collectors, often end up stored in bank vaults like so many negotiable bonds, or exhibited in circumstances where nobody can study them in tolerable comfort and tranquillity.

These problems – theft and pillage, speculation and over-valuation, the demands of the museum and the crowd – are all manifestations of the curious form our reverence for art has taken, and are so closely related that they must be considered interdependent. Destruction and abuse in the name of art, and the artificial inflation of values which puts fine objects beyond the reach of those who might enjoy them, together constitute what I call the art crisis.

My aim in this book has been to show how the various elements of art collecting and marketing – both legal and illegal – contribute to this crisis; and how the situation in turn feeds on itself by stimulating the continuation and growth of the same activities as produced it. The art crisis resembles such other well-known contemporary phenomena as the energy crisis or the environmental crisis. A long-standing disregard for an asset which has hitherto been in reasonably good supply has led to a laxity in our treatment of it. Then a sudden demand has produced shortages and shortage, exploitation of what is left. The art crisis is something in which we all participate and which only a general change of consciousness will alter.

The book is divided into three sections: the first considers art theft in its various forms; the second the clouded moral problem of the antiquities market; the third the commercialization of art. The first two sections thus are concerned with the illicit means through which art objects are obtained and brought to the market; the third deals with art as mass entertainment and investment, and the stimulus that these roles give to the abuse of the culture that provides their *raison d'être*.

My own involvement with this problem began in 1971 when I started working for the International Council of Museums (ICOM) in Paris as special coordinator for a project called Ethics of Acquisition, a campaign against the acquisition by museums of smuggled antiquities and undocumented art.

When I started my work on the ICOM project, my viewpoint was similar to that of most of the museum people I knew. I felt that the museum's job was to collect and preserve art, that anything on the market was fit to be collected so long as its quality warranted its being placed in a museum.

At ICOM I began to see the problem of acquisition from the other side. Dealings with officials from the poor but 'art-rich' countries made me aware of the validity of those countries' claims to their own art, and of their inability to protect their heritage. Even more important, I became aware of the destruction and desecration that were being carried out in the name of art, and of the damage that resulted from museums seeking to accumulate all the art of high quality to be found anywhere in the world.

When I had finished my work on the ICOM project, I decided

to write this book – a book that would set forth the broader implications of the problem, as it affected the intelligent layman who was interested in art, as well as the potential art buyer. At this point, my feelings on the issue changed, as I began to see the scope of the dilemma, and to discover that even those whose ethical position seemed most equivocal felt a real concern for what was happening.

I have tried, in writing this book, to avoid falling into all-too-easy condemnations of one party or another. It has not been my purpose to plead for or against any particular viewpoint, but rather to show the enormity and complexity of the problem; perhaps in some cases also to give the reader some idea of the factors which may surround his decision to purchase or not to purchase a work of art.

Is it indeed possible to buy art without getting involved in the vicious circle of pillage and destruction? Can one hope to change the direction or slow the pace of this trend? These are the questions which prompted me to write this book, and which I hope the book will help to illuminate if not to answer.

Many of the phenomena discussed in this book will be familiar to the reader, through a number of incidents – such as the scandal over the Metropolitan Museum's acquisition of the Euphronius calyx krater, the looting of antiquities in Latin America, and certain celebrated art thefts – which, in the past few years, have drawn public attention to this issue. Many such incidents I have omitted from the present work, or mentioned only in passing, on the assumption that they were already well known, and would yield little new from being further probed. Instead, I have concentrated, in almost every chapter, on a single event or situation which I know well, in order to point the existence of a larger problem. Likewise, I have avoided dwelling on the local efforts that are being made to check this problem, or on the technical and legal aspects of the protection of cultural property. This is because of my conviction that the art crisis should be recognized as a social problem, which will only be dealt with successfully when the governments of the world, and their citizens, become aware of its significance.

Although I have tried to give a fair picture, the book is not without its prejudices. I have striven for objectivity in my presentation of the facts, but have not been able to avoid colouring them with my own evaluation of what they mean. After the time I have spent working as a professional in the field, it could not be otherwise. I do not ask the reader to accept all my opinions as valid, nor all my judgements as correct, but merely to keep in mind the incidents presented in this book when he finally judges for himself. The problems with which the book deals are too important to be resolved by mere slogans and propaganda.

Part I

STOLEN ART

I

THE FLIGHT FROM TOURS

Anatomy of an Art Theft

Housed in the majestic seventeeth-century archbishop's palace, the Tours art museum is one of the lovely, well-kept museums of which provincial European cities are so proud. The wood floors of its galleries are highly polished, and the paintings, surrounded by period furniture and the rich aroma of fresh wax, occupy the generous space in a way that at once maintains some of the sense of a palace and also invites the visitor to feel at home. The museum overlooks a fine formal garden, surrounded by a high stone wall, which separates the mansion from the Cathedral square.

One of the jewels of the museum's collection is the small but masterful early Rembrandt *Flight into Egypt*, the earliest known work in which Rembrandt experimented with a dramatic contrast of dark and light. Until the painting was given to the Tours museum in 1950, it was virtually unknown, and had not been recognized as a work by Rembrandt. Within the next few years, however, its singularity within the development of Rembrandt's style had made it well known. It was exhibited at the Stockholm and Leyden Rembrandt exhibitions in 1956, and subsequently travelled to a number of loan exhibitions, including the Paris 'Century of Rembrandt' show in the winter of 1970–71.

Less than a year after the painting returned from Paris, on 21 December 1971, it had added to its history the dubious distinction of being the last important art work stolen in 1971 – a peak year for the theft of masterpieces.

For people concerned about art, 1971 seemed like a long nightmare of theft and senseless destruction. In March of that year three Rembrandts had been stolen from the Musée Bonnat in Bayonne, France. The same month the famous *Virgin and Child*, one of a handful of extant paintings by the fifteenth-century master Masaccio, and a small portrait by Hans Memling were stolen from a closed room in the Palazzo Vecchio in Florence. In May, someone even had the audacity to steal a large sculpture by Tine from the open terrace of the Museum of Modern Art in Paris. Then in June, five seventeenth-century paintings and two statues, valued at over 5 million Belgian francs (about £50,000), disappeared from the château of Denise Rolin at Knokke-Heist; a polyptych of seven panels was stolen from the cathedral of Brescia, Italy, and the Prado Museum in Madrid recorded the loss of a tiny but priceless Jan van Kessel oil on copper painting.

During the summer holiday months, art burglaries of unoccupied apartments and villas were daily news; the thieves going after both important and minor works. Then in August, northern Italy seemed to have gone mad with what the newspapers termed 'artnapping' – the stealing of art for ransom. One of the first victims was the great Titian *Holy Conversation*, the only work by the master still found in his native town of Pieve de Cavone, near Padua. It was stolen from the village's parish church, along with thirteen other paintings, and held for a large ransom. The thieves, who turned out to be peasants from a nearby village, were caught in a police trap while trying to collect the ransom. The paintings were recovered unharmed.

Shortly afterwards, two large paintings by Giovanni Bellini and a triptych by Vivarini were found to be missing from the church of SS Giovanni e Paolo in Venice. Again the thieves offered the works back for ransom. After lengthy secret negotiations, a ransom of approximately 5 million lira ($8000) was paid, and the police were told where to find the paintings, which had been abandoned on one of the deserted islands outside Venice. The recovered works were found to be damaged, but not beyond repair, and the thieves – minor local criminals – were eventually caught.

By the early autumn, the situation in Italy had begun to be reflected throughout Europe. Statistics rolling in from police forces all over the continent showed that 1971 was shaping up as the biggest year in the history of art theft. That September twenty tiny panels from a fourteenth-century altarpiece were dismantled overnight and stolen from the Paris church of St Nicolas des Champs. Only three months before, in the same church, an angel had been sliced from a large canvas attributed to the seventeenth-century French artist Le Sueur. That September was also the date of one of the most vicious assaults to date on a work of art. The celebrated Vermeer *Love Letter* was hacked from its frame and stolen on the opening night of an important exhibition in Brussels. The motive was again extortion, only this time the impetus was political. The 22-year-old thief demanded a ransom of 200 million Belgian francs ($4.8 million), to be contributed to the cause of Bengali refugees. Although the painting was eventually recovered, it had been horribly defaced.

The defacement of the Vermeer provoked much public outrage and a dispute over who was responsible for allowing such events to happen. The police were blamed for incompetence, the museums for indifference. Legislators called on their respective governments to allocate more money for the protection of art; the Belgian government made an urgent appeal to UNESCO. In Venice, it was announced that all paintings presently in churches would be removed to museums for better security. But it was impossible to anticipate where thieves would next strike.

At a moment when airline hijackings and terrorism made the headlines almost every day, these senseless art thefts seemed to affirm the presence of a growing, destructive madness in the world. It began to become apparent that the psychological barrier which had traditionally protected establishments that house art, and made well-known works virtually unstealable, could no longer be depended upon.

The theft of the Tours Rembrandt was a case in point. Although it might be unfair to say that the staff of the Tours museum had never given much thought to security, the subject had evidently been approached as it is by many small museums – as a curatorial concern of secondary importance. The beautiful building and peaceful garden, the giant cedar in the courtyard, and the quiet galleries hung with damask and paintings – by Fouquet, Mantegna, Rubens and Rembrandt among others – must have seemed incapable of inspiring any destructive act. The idea that the building's tall windows, with their ornate closings and ancient rippled panes could invite burglary as well as admiration seems not to have troubled anyone. Nor did anyone consider that the stone wall which encloses the building and its park might serve as a challenge rather than a deterrent to a modern burglar. The Tours museum had no night guard, no insurance, and no alarm system of any kind. Although this may seem like an outrageous oversight, it is in fact quite normal. Because of the considerable cost of such precautions most of the world's museums are in a similar position. Traditionally, the museum has depended heavily upon the fact that it is a museum to protect it from abuse by the public.

The Tours museum is built next to the cathedral, with its back to the cathedral's south side. Here the building comes closest to the wall, separated from it by a narrow space of about ten feet, which is filled with one-storey, flat-roofed outbuildings. On the night of 21 December 1971, the thief chose this point to climb the wall, using a ladder borrowed from the restoration work being done on the cathedral next door. He crossed the roof of the outbuilding, broke one pane of the single accessible window, reached through, lifted the latch and opened the window. When he climbed in, he found himself in the room where the Dutch master paintings were hung. He took two – the tiny Rembrandt, only 9×10 inches large, yet valued at 700,000 francs ($140,000), and an ordinary seascape by the seventeenth-century Dutch painter Van Goyen. The later events of the story suggest that he chose this second painting under the mistaken impression that it was a Van Gogh. He left the museum by the way he had come, without causing any other disorder and without leaving a clue.

Next morning the museum guards discovered the open window and missing paintings. The local police were informed and a preliminary investigation was made. There were no clues. The case was then handed over to Jacques-Paul Mathieu, head of a special Paris police unit formed in 1970 to deal primarily with the growing problem of art thefts.

For Mathieu's unit, the Tours theft was what one might call a routine museum case. The paintings were uninsured, which meant that there would be no help on the case from a special investigator, hired by an insurance company (which is the only body which has any financial interest in seeing the art returned to its owner). There were no leads or clues found by the local police, and after a few days with no contact it seemed unlikely that the theft was a ransom attempt. Normal contacts in the underworld yielded no information. The police reached the conclusion that the thief was probably a relative amateur, working alone.

At this point, the case was cold. Although the police had trimmed down the list of possible motives, the art squad knew little more about the Tours museum theft than the average reader who learned about it from the newspapers. It was hoped that the case (and the paintings) would be saved by the notoriety surrounding the Rembrandt. Such notoriety would certainly discourage most dealers from getting involved with the painting, and would perhaps result in some cooperation from authorities abroad, where the paintings were likely to turn up.

Mathieu immediately sent photographs and descriptions of the stolen paintings to Interpol, which would rapidly diffuse this information around the world. The press was also helping in this process – even the smallest notice is significant in making a theft internationally known. Aside from this, there was nothing that could be done. The police estimate that most stolen paintings go abroad or underground within twenty-four hours of a theft. After a week, there is little to do but wait for the next clue.

Art squads now exist in the capitals of all the major Western countries. Mathieu's unit in Paris consists of seven men who share the double burden of computerizing all the information they can obtain about art thefts everywhere, and of solving cases under their own jurisdiction. Like art squads all over the world, they also spend a good deal of their energy developing and perfecting new methods of operation, and even justifying their work to the rest of the police. For, curiously enough, the goals of the art squads are somewhat at odds with those of the regular police.

The main function of the police is to arrest criminals, to stop crime. Recovery of merchandise is a secondary activity, a mere follow-up to the apprehension of offenders. For an art squad, on the other hand, recovering the stolen art objects is of primary importance – even if the recovery does not lead to an arrest or a 'solved' crime. This makes the art squad's performance difficult to evaluate in terms of the usual criteria such as crime prevention and number of arrests. It also requires the art detective to develop a specialized approach to his work, for which his police training provides little preparation.

While the regular detective usually has an indispensable network of underworld informers, a great deal of the art squad's success depends on contacts in the strangely incomprehensible art world, and upon systematic recording and storing of information. This latter task, which is important in solving all kinds of thefts involving internationally-negotiable merchandise, is particularly essential to art recovery. But much to the disadvantage of art squads everywhere, it is a task that has been largely neglected until recently.

Although Interpol has maintained a listing of internationally-sought stolen art for over thirty years, officers of the organization estimate that this listing contains, at most, only about one third of all the art that is stolen in the world. Because of the high cost and enormous work involved in circulating stolen art bulletins, Interpol must discourage countries from sending them reports of art thefts unless there is strong evidence that the objects have been taken abroad. The principal task of Interpol is to diffuse news of an important theft when it is reported to them, not to maintain a definitive listing of stolen objects. Elsewhere, police departments have been keeping systematic records of local thefts for less than five years, and have no way of exchanging this information regularly.

In addition, only about thirty per cent of the objects stolen have ever been photographed. This means not only that stolen works are often practically unidentifiable, but also that when a work suspected of being stolen turns up on the market, the police often cannot prove that it *was* stolen, or from where. One day I went to Interpol and found their art theft specialist Robert Sauger thumbing through the thick books which list stolen paintings, looking for a 'Picasso'. A cable from England established that two Picassos, suspected of being stolen in Germany, were in the hands of a black market vendor. No photographs were available. Sauger's investigation was fruitless. He found listings for a number of stolen Picassos, but none from Germany. And the description of the pictures in England was not detailed enough to establish whether the two Picassos might have been stolen elsewhere.

The difficult task of the art squads is thus magnified by the fact that they are heavily dependent for their success on information that is often faulty or incomplete. Art recoveries result more often from recognition of a stolen object when it is offered for sale than from tracking a thief. Stolen art will generally pass back into the circuit of the regular market. Paintings cannot, like other merchandise, be broken down, dispersed, or disguised; and even objects with a concrete material value, like silver candlesticks and diamond tiaras, must be saleable *as is* in order to realize the value that made them targets for the thief. It is upon this fact that most art theft investigations depend. For the majority of unknown, unphotographed objects, there is little hope of a recovery. For a well-documented work there is near certainty that the police will eventually come across a trace. This is how the next lead developed in the case of the Tours Rembrandt.

Late in February 1972 the German police in Wiesbaden reported to Interpol what seemed like the first breakthrough in the case. A painting thought to be the stolen Rembrandt and a 'Van Gogh' had been offered, and the police thought sold, to a dealer in Berlin. The telegram specified that the seller was an unknown man of Czech nationality, and ended by stating enigmatically that the two paintings had been in Berlin for a few days, but then had disappeared, and were presumed to be 'destined for the market in South America'.

The mention of South America, a recurrent one in art theft accounts, introduced an ominous note into the Tours case. If, for the general public, South America evokes the image of desperados, Mafiosi and mad millionaires, to the police it signifies an exasperating uncooperativeness which can effectively halt their investigations. The French art squad had already had one encounter that year with South American law enforcement. They had received word of a huge cache of stolen European paintings, discovered in the home of a gangster in Brazil. This, they felt, might prove that a tie-up existed between art stealing and international organized crime. Urgent messages were sent asking for descriptions of the objects confiscated, but the other end of the wire was silent. No reply was ever received.

South American justice has a reputation for following its own rules. Criminals and political refugees are protected from extradition, and stolen treasures, of whatever value, are secluded behind a barrier of non-communication between these states and the rest of the world. The warning that a painting has been sent to South America therefore carries the implication that it has disappeared into a vacuum, never to return. If the Tours Rembrandt was in fact on its way to South America, the painting could be considered, for all practical purposes, lost.

But before the South America rumour could be investigated, the German police had new information. They sent a cable to Paris asking whether the French had ever heard of one Karl Whitman, a 22-year-old youth of Czechoslovak origin, who was at that time in Germany and was thought to be offering the Tours paintings. The French made a check and by the end of March learned that in 1971 Whitman had indeed been living in Tours. The case seemed to be gaining momentum and Whitman was watched, then brought in for questioning by the German police. Yes, Whitman confirmed, he had lived in Tours during 1971 and travelled in Germany since; but no, he had never stolen a Rembrandt. No trace of the paintings themselves could be found.

The two messages from Germany indicated that the thief had surfaced, and was seeking a buyer. Whitman had been traced to Berlin and to Dusseldorf, where he was presumed to have offered the paintings around. The questioning of Whitman, however, by letting him know that he was under suspicion, added a new factor to the case. If Whitman was in actual possession of the paintings, he might decide to hide them, pass them on to another vendor, or even destroy them, for fear of arrest. On the other hand, the police pressure might make him realize that he had stolen something a little hotter than he had imagined, and induce him to abandon the merchandise and tip off the police – the outcome of many over-ambitious art thefts. Which, if any, of these courses a thief in this position might follow would depend on several factors: whether he had good connections in the black market; how worried he was about being caught; how urgently he needed money.

After questioning Whitman, the German police, concerned for the safety of the paintings, relaxed their surveillance. A telegram came into Interpol in June 1972 reiterating the suspicion that Karl Whitman was the thief. Then there was nothing.

During the summer of 1972, while the French and German police were carefully probing for the Tours Rembrandt, a new kind of 'wanted' poster appeared, featuring not celebrated criminals, but the world's Twelve Most Wanted Works of Art. In June 1972, Interpol and the International Council of Museums (ICOM) collaborated to produce the first of these listings, in an effort to draw greater professional attention to the world-wide increase in art theft. The large illustrated posters, featuring some of the finest paintings in the world, made a great psychological impression. They reminded dealers of the imminent possibility and unpleasant consequences of buying stolen art, and brought the problem dramatically to the public. More important, they would perhaps deter potential art stealers from getting involved in crime which received such serious attention from Interpol. '*C'est bien*,' Jacques-Paul Mathieu exclaimed, '*et surtout c'est spectaculaire*.'

The impact of the posters was so great that, in November 1972, Interpol decided to institutionalize the idea of Most Wanted Art, and produced a second sheet of 'most wanted' paintings, which appeared in newspapers around the world. On it was the Tours Rembrandt.

Almost simultaneously came the next big break in the case. In mid-November, the curator of the Tours museum received an anonymous telephone call. A woman's voice offered the Rembrandt against a ransom of 30,000 DM. The curator notified the police and, when the second call came, a rendezvous was set in Saarbrucken to negotiate the painting's return. This new development indicated that the thief, after unsuccessfully trying to negotiate the sale of the painting, was making a run for it. Offering the Rembrandt for ransom was a move of desperation – a signal of defeat.

Almost a year had passed since the theft, ample time for a buyer to be found, if one was forthcoming. The police had been on the trail of the suspected thief for months, and the worldwide publication of the painting as a most wanted work of art would greatly diminish the chance of negotiating a sale, even on the black market, for many years to come. The ransom call told the police something very important. The thief had nowhere to go with the painting, had not sent it abroad, and would risk a chance of being caught rather than abandon or destroy it. Things were coming to a head. Then suddenly Whitman was arrested in Germany for another theft, apprehended at the Berlin airport as he tried to leave the country. But Whitman would not confess to the theft of the Rembrandt, and no longer had the paintings.

Some time early in 1972 he had given them to a Dusseldorf middleman for handling. The middleman had sold the Van Goyen to a dealer in Berlin, who in turn sold it again. But over the Rembrandt, the dealer seemed to be hesitating. The Van Goyen, being only a minor seascape in a minor painter's *oeuvre*, had been easy to sell on the black market. To sell the Rembrandt, however, was a different matter. Perhaps the asking price, reported at one point to be as high as 100,000 DM ($31,000) was too high; the going resale rate for a stolen painting is rarely more than 10–20 per cent of its value, and the painting was worth around 400,000 DM. Perhaps police discovery seemed imminent, or the dealer was seeking an immediate buyer before taking on such a notorious work of art. There was, at any rate, some chance that the sale would not materialize, and the middleman was rapidly becoming impatient to dispose of the piece. He decided to take the more dangerous tack of negotiating a ransom for its return.

A meeting to begin the ransom negotiations was arranged for six o'clock on the evening of 2nd December, 1972, at the restaurant of the Saarbrucken railway station. Details had been carefully worked out between the ransom negotiator and the authorities. A representative of the museum would meet a woman negotiator who would identify herself by wearing a brown leather coat and carrying a copy of the Paris newspaper *l'Aurore*. The two of them would decide on a price and discuss the details of the return in the anonymity of the railway station restaurant.

The police of course had made additional preparations. The restaurant was filled with undercover agents dining with their wives. A motion picture camera was installed on a nearby roof, to photograph the ransom negotiator. And finally, the train that arrived from France at 5.51 would not be carrying a representative of the museum, but a police agent posing as that representative.

But a series of odd coincidences forced the police to change their plans. At 5.30 a woman entered the railway station, wearing a brown leather coat. At the newsstand she asked for a copy of *l'Aurore*, but was told that there were no more. Somewhat unnerved by this, she bought another French newspaper instead. As she left the kiosk, a man who had been seen shortly before in the restaurant approached her, and took her arm. They talked for a moment, and then she disappeared on foot into the centre of town. Her accomplice waited a few minutes and then, convinced that she was not being followed, he too headed into town.

The man and woman met in a downtown car park where they picked up a car. From there they drove to the nearby town of Kirkel. At this point, the police lost track of them, but they caught sight of the car again later that evening, parked in front of a house in Kirkel. At almost the same time, the Saarbrucken police received a phone call. The caller asked to speak with the person in charge of the Saarbrucken railway station case, and declared that he and his wife were the negotiators. He asked for an appointment the next morning to discuss the business, but was persuaded by the police to meet them the same night.

The negotiator told the police that his wife had been persuaded, for personal reasons, to seek a buyer for the paintings. The price was 100,000 DM. He said the identity of the person selling the paintings was unknown to them. At the Saarbrucken station, the man had become suspicious when shortly before his wife's arrival, he too had tried to buy a copy of *l'Aurore* at the newsstand. The vendor had explained to him agitatedly that she had been out of *l'Aurore* since 4.20, and asked him if he was from the police. He had realized from this that a trap had been set.

At the time of his conversation with the police, the negotiator was still sure that he could arrange the return of the painting, against 100,000 DM, on which he would receive a commission. He told the police that he could delay his negotiations as long as the 6th of December, while the museum raised the money. The painting, he explained, was nowhere at hand.

By this time, the number of people suspected to be implicated in the affair had risen to five or six. There was the alleged thief and his girlfriend, who was also thought to have had a part in the theft. There was the middleman, the middleman's agent, and the Berlin dealer. The police had before them the seemingly impossible task of getting together the middleman and the Rembrandt, capturing the Rembrandt, arresting the middleman, recovering any ransom money that might have been paid, and discovering the whereabouts of and seizing the Van Goyen as well.

A meeting was arranged in Berlin for the 13th of December, almost exactly a year after the theft, and just one month after Interpol's bulletin had appeared naming the Tours Rembrandt among the world's most wanted works of art. The Saarbrucken agent arranged an interview in Berlin, to be held exclusively with the Tours museum's representative. If the police intervened, he warned, the painting would not be returned. Nevertheless it was a member of the Paris art squad who boarded the plane to Berlin, to arrange the final meeting and recover the Rembrandt. On the plane, he opened his newspaper and read, 'Rembrandt *Flight into Egypt* recovered in West Berlin'. The job had been completed before he arrived.

The middleman had made one last effort to sell the painting, perhaps hoping to keep all the money for himself, and not pay his Saarbrucken agent. He had approached the Berlin dealer again. This time, the police, having learned the middleman's identity, were there for the delivery. They recovered the Rembrandt and, after questioning the dealer, managed to seize the Van Goyen as well. The case was closed.

Or so it might have seemed.

A year after the recovery of the paintings, I went to Tours to speak to the curator of the museum. Much to my surprise, I learned that the painting had still not been returned. The curator, who had also learned of its recovery from the newspaper, had been able to learn very little since. She told me that she knew nothing about the state of conservation of the two delicate panel paintings, nor exactly where or how the paintings were being stored. She assumed that a legal technicality prevented their being returned before the trial of the thief. She was concerned for the safety of the paintings, but did not know what to do. She encouraged me not to publish any account of the affair, and indeed refused to talk about the ransom call – assuming that all art thefts eventually end in a ransom call and the recovery of the painting. (*Ils sont tous comme ça, Mais ça n'a rien d'extraordinaire.*) As we talked, she suggested that the International Council of Museums might help by seeing that such stolen works were properly cared for after their recovery.

When I later called on Jacques-Paul Mathieu to ask whether such an intervention would be helpful, he explained that the question was far more simple. The recovery of the painting was the responsibility of the owner. Often, he said with amusement, private collectors liked to accompany the police when their paintings were to be recovered, so anxious were they to get the paintings back and to see that they were safely handled. In the case of a museum work, owned by the public, it was up to the government.

At this point the government still had not decided what to do. At the Musées de France, the responsibility to get the painting back had automatically passed to the administration of Provincial Museums, and the recovery of the Rembrandt had apparently lost priority. And at his own office, Mathieu was too short of funds to undertake anything that was not strictly necessary. To date, Mathieu explained, neither his office nor the administration of the Musées de France had found the money to send someone to pick the paintings up.

Ironically, this fact had caused another complication. Whitman, the alleged thief, had served his German sentence for another crime and had been extradited to France in October 1973, to stand trial for the theft of the Tours paintings. The trial would be held in Tours, but could not take place until the paintings were back from Germany.

The legal commission in charge of the trial might now take on the responsibility of arranging for the paintings' return, Mathieu told me. Otherwise, it would have to wait.

After another six months had passed, I again telephoned the Tours museum to learn the fate of the stolen Rembrandt. The paintings had been brought back to France and were being held at the Louvre, I was told, for an indefinite period. The museum's curator would not comment on the reason for their retention there, or on when the Rembrandt could again be seen in Tours.

It should therefore be a moment for some celebration when the *Flight into Egypt* has concluded its own flight and is back in its place in the museum, all the more notorious and valuable since the theft. During its absence, the museum has installed an alarm system to prevent future break-ins, and the small panel paintings have, sadly but wisely, been put inside a locked show-case, which is also wired to the alarm. This museum has learned the hard way that psychological protection no longer suffices, and that nothing is unstealable, certainly no work of art.

The art thefts which have involved many famous paintings in recent years are for the most part variations on this story. Although the reader may be surprised to find that someone with no ex-perience or contacts in the art world would steal an important painting, this is usually the case. Newsworthy art thefts are generally committed either by local people attracted by the celebrity of a work of art to which they have easy access, or by people involved in other kinds of crime. The thefts are often solved when the criminal is arrested for something else: the famous Schongauer *Virgin of the Rosebush* was recovered in the summer of 1973 from a garage where it was hidden by a gangster who had meanwhile gone to jail for armed robbery and shooting a policeman; the modern paintings stolen from the French financier Robert Frenkel were found in the apartment of a man involved in a bank robbery.

If the chances of successfully stealing and negotiating a well-known art object seem small enough to discourage a criminal without connections in the art world, it must be remembered that the profits to be made are great and that, because of the minimal protection provided for art collections everywhere, the dangers at the time of the theft are ridiculously small. Furthermore, for every recovered painting there are a dozen less important works which are not recovered. They become part of the merchandise of the underworld market and are sold for a fraction of their value. (The price is established by reading newspaper accounts after the theft, which almost always note the value of the stolen work. Lacking this, the middleman consults an art auction catalogue!) Works of art pass from intermediary to intermediary, usually out of the country where they were stolen, until they eventually find a permanent resting place. Although several of Interpol's original Twelve Most Wanted masterpieces have now been recovered, there are many more objects which will never be returned. And the number and variety of art thefts and thieves keeps increasing.

2

DEALERS AND WHEELER-DEALERS

The Black Market in Art

If art recovery is a sometimes thing, this is not only because inefficiency and lack of funds handicap the work. A large proportion of art thefts are committed by professionals who supply the black market in art, a tightly organized business operation which is all the more efficient for being excellently camouflaged within the honest trade. This underground market not only takes advantage of loopholes in the law, it also profits from the tradition of secrecy and discretion maintained by art dealers in general.

A wide range of people earn their living as dealers in art, and they have varying viewpoints on how to deal and on what is ethical. The use of the term 'art dealer' is perhaps too broad. A financial empire like Marlborough Fine Arts of London, with branches everywhere and a high reputation for sponsoring artists and contributing to scholarship, has little in common with a side-street gallery which closes and moves from one neighbourhood or town to another, towing along whatever works of art it might have on consignment (too bad for the artist or lender who cannot track them down). Yet they share the same generic name and reputation.

In fact, a reputation for marginally unethical transactions, for internecine spying, for tampering with one another's trade, is studiously cultivated by many dealers, merely for the sake of glamour. The image in its contemporary form was created by the brilliant career of Lord Duveen, who managed the incredible coup of having his clients vie for his favours: 'You are not ready for a Duveen,' he would say to a millionaire who wanted to get into the vogue of collecting. And the clients to whom he did condescend to sell (whose fortunes were sometimes inferior to his own, made exclusively in dealing), had to pass many tests before they merited being sold a *great* Duveen.

Today, both dealers with the most modest holdings and powerful high-pressure galleries use the psychology, by now institutionalized, that was invented by Duveen. In virtually every encounter with a dealer, one meets the same references to his unique intelligence network, the same reluctance to talk about the sources of the art he sells, the same heady gossip, in which hints are dropped so that the informed listener can deduce to whom the stories refer. In almost every gallery the buyer meets the same aloof snobbery and is alternately baited and tantalized in a ritual way. This tends to give the average buyer the impression that dealers are all engaged in the same practice, which is utterly untrue. There is more than one art market, and there are different levels of integrity in both open and private dealing.

There are two kinds of dealers involved in the illegal art trade. One might be the proprietor of a small Chelsea antique shop or 3rd Avenue junk shop, a flea market *brocanteur*; the other a hazy figure who maintains no gallery and operates from his home. In the case of the small antique or junk dealer, it is easy to see how a struggling business might become tied up with the black market. As one passes these shops and sees the same merchandise for sale, month after month, or moving around the quarter, going from one dealer to another up and down the Fulham Road, one wonders how there can possibly be a living in the trade. Many of these dealers must supplement their gallery income with odd jobs – restorations, buying for a collector at an auction, interior decorating. A few others make up their losses by dealing in inconspicuous stolen objects. The dealer's shop provides a convenient front – the arrival and departure of large quantities of art attracts no particular notice. The objects are low-priced; the dealer can buy them for about 10 per cent of their worth, or take them on consignment, paying nothing until he makes a sale. Once set up in the trade, there is an almost constant flow of art coming from churches and châteaux all over Europe. Uninsured, unphotographed, and often unmentioned in the press, these stolen objects make up a lucrative business. With the quantity of freight being shipped today, there is no problem with transport. The objects pass so easily that the process can scarcely be called smuggling.

Occasionally a large international operation is discovered and broken up by the police. When the Chelsea dealer William Horan was arrested in 1972 for handling stolen art, he had £100,000 worth of stolen merchandise in his possession. Some of it would conceivably have been redispatched to other dealers on the circuit, as was a painting by Juncker, stolen from Hampton Court, which was recovered in Brussels at the time of the arrest; other objects might simply have been sold over the counter, or disposed of anonymously at auction.

It seems that little restriction can be put on this trade, although governments have tried. In France, there is a law which requires merchants to register every transaction over 10,000 francs ($2000). listing the name of the buyer or seller, and the price paid. Payments to art sellers should be made by certified cheque, delivered to the seller's domicile. According to this law, it would be possible to establish where a work of art came from and, when a stolen work turned up, to trace the seller and establish whether the dealer had constant dealings with him. But this law has functioned poorly. A few years ago, when restraints on peripheral economic activities were tightened and the government attempted to enforce this law, it was reportedly confronted by a united coalition of dealers who asserted that the authority must either put them all in jail, or forget about their plan. The government apparently did the latter, and the art market has continued without other regular restraint. The only real sanction against these marginal dealers has been the formation of antique dealers' and art dealers' associations, whose members are carefully chosen because they have a reputable standing and abide by certain ethics. Such associations were formed partly to eliminate the more undesirable elements of the trade. In many countries, however, they still do not exist, and in France the *Comité Professionnel des Galeries* has no code of ethics, and is uniquely a prestige and conference organization.

More sensational and more important than the small dealers who participate occasionally in the black market are the brokers and private dealers whose activities pass under a veil of secrecy so dense that it is almost impossible to define either the range or the extent of their trade. Within this category there is a variety of personalities and types. The reputation of the trade is improved by the fact that members of Europe's noblest families indulge in it, as do some former scholars, archaeologists, and museum curators – disillusioned by the ineffectualness and bureaucracy that invaded their professional careers. Many private dealers have significant financial resources behind them, a high level of expertise, and great personal taste. Others are *demi-monde* figures for whom dealing in art is a *raison social*, an opportunity to ingratiate oneself into the best society. Some private dealers sell to and counsel rich men, and become rich themselves; others are merely brokers who buy something for a collector and are paid a commission, or who buy an object and resell it immediately to another, more important dealer – they are agents, intermediaries; many of them, despite their showy fronts, live on the verge of starvation.

In New York, they are often businessmen who have made fortunes in commerce and have become jaded. They turn their attention from merely collecting art to trading in it – for amusement, and because of the high prices paid for art today. And, of course, many of them have brought their sharp business methods to the art world.

Why do aristocrats or distinguished collectors and scholars become art dealers? One private dealer put it to me this way: 'Suppose your consuming passion is *haute cuisine*, but you don't have the resources to eat at Maxim's. What do you do? Become professionally involved with food, become a cook. But making fish and chips day after day has no relationship to *haute cuisine*. If you love good food, you have no choice but to become a great chef.' The private dealer is the *grand chef de cuisine* of the art market. Many of the most lucrative transactions in the art world are carried out at his level. These dealers make it a point to know the whereabouts of available works, and to keep up with what is going on around them. Their business constitutes an important trade, and its success poses a certain threat to the open market.

The private dealer does not operate by the accepted rules of the profession. He has no gallery and keeps no stock of paintings for sale, nor is he required to make the 'satisfaction guarantees' that the gallery is held to. The private dealer's job is to 'serve clients', either by disposing of paintings for them, or by providing them with works they might want to buy.

On the whole, they love the sport and danger of the marginally illicit trade, are vague about the nature of their operations, and delight in making provocative statements that intensify their mystery.

'Now a £50,000 transaction cannot be very interesting. A £1 million transaction, that's what interests me,' one such dealer told me.

They place no limitations on the range of their work:

'Do you specialize?'

'I specialize in making money. I am a merchant.'

'What kind of art do you sell?'

'What have you heard I sell?'

(A certain sale is mentioned.)

'Yes, I sold that.'

'Do you buy at auctions?'

'Have you ever seen me there?'

'What do you collect?'

'I don't.'

'What did you study?'

'Byzantine art. At a place called the Courtauld Institute.'

'Do you buy and sell Byzantine art?'

'Only if somebody pays me to – pays me well.'

They live in comfortable opulence, either surrounded by the objects which their passion has led them to trade in, or with such objects conspicuously absent from their decors. One private dealer I met has no art on his walls, but has a framed picture of a coiled cobra hanging over his desk. *Caveat Emptor.*

Many private dealers are scrupulously professional men with fine sensibilities. Such dealers offer excellent opportunities for the collector to dispose of an object quietly, or for an amateur to avoid the dupery, snobbery and vulgarity that are often associated with art galleries. The private dealer, since he is not obliged to maintain large stocks, mount dazzling exhibitions, cater to preferred clients, or follow trends, can work on instinct and deal in a wide range of articles. He works like a lawyer, disposing of a collection for a fixed commission. No consignment, no partial sales or strung-out payments, as one often has when dealing with a gallery. The private dealer can usually negotiate a higher price than would be got at auction. If auction prices are rising, they still do not reflect what is paid for art. Private dealers sell to rich men. They sell dear. Or they sell on the market, using all their accumulated experience to take advantage of an upward fluctuation. The private dealer, with few other concerns, can afford to use his wits.

But the existence of the bona fide private dealer also provides his less scrupulous colleague with a respectable cover. A man can call himself a broker when his dealings are in reality the theft and fencing of stolen art. One of the easiest ways to make a huge profit on art is to steal it and resell it.

The urban broker rarely involves himself directly in the mechanics of a theft. He places a commission for a certain work of art with a middleman, who may be a shop-owner, a small-time art dealer, or even, as in several recent cases, an undertaker: a respectable member of the community who is also an art fence. This man operates a string of youths who are making their debut in the underworld and who commit the thefts. These youths, I was told by one ex-art thief, call him their 'Fagin' – in due honour to the memory of Dickens. The dealer contacts the Fagin, who arranges the theft with a professional contact.

The thief begins to make rounds. He 'lays on the place'. To discover the particular quirks of the establishment to be robbed, he checks and analyses the alarm system, memorizes the movements of the members of the household, gets to know the guard. He goes to the public library and looks up in art books the thing to be stolen. The price paid by the dealer will be split between himself and the Fagin. He makes good use of the advances in art scholarship in establishing for his own information the importance of the work and its value – this also allows him to establish whether the commission he is getting is satisfactory. The Fagin will get 10–25 per cent of the total commission price – but by the time a getaway arrangement is made (a commissioned driver is called a 'wheel man') the thief gets only about half. ('The Fagin gets as much as you do,' I was told.) The experience of the thief and the technique with which the job is done determine the thief's portion. ('You rip the painting, they lower your pay,' my contact explained.) The thief uses his own inventiveness to decide how the theft will be carried out. The best way to steal a Greek vase from a museum, I was told, is to put it in a bag filled with popcorn and drop it out the window. The popcorn protects it from shattering, is easier to secure than Styrofoam, and raises less suspicion. When robbing a private house, an umbrella taken from the hall will conceal a rolled-up canvas. It is better to use an umbrella found in the house than to bring one, for the thief wants to look as anonymous as possible before the theft; a man carrying an umbrella is easier for a passer-by to remember than a man without one.

An important museum job may be worth a nocturnal visit to the company which insures the collection, and whose records contain detailed plans of the museum lay-out, with the burglar-alarm system and its electronic circuits marked. One art thief told me that he would hesitate to burgle a private home in the summer, when the inhabitants were away, there being a chance that as a protective measure the paintings on the walls would have been replaced by copies. (In an ironic reverse of this practice, a collector in France is said to have recently made copies to replace the paintings on his walls during his holidays. Then, satisfied with the copies he had ordered, he arranged to have the copies stolen, and collected the insurance, while keeping the original paintings.) There are thieves who leave behind some symbol of their passing, or take along a memento. In the theft from Sir Roland Penrose's house in London in 1968, an old broken-down typewriter disappeared along with eight important impressionist paintings.

The thief and the merchandise usually part company immediately after the theft. The goods are deposited in the car of the wheel man who brings them to the fence. The fence maintains a tight grip on the whole operation, and on everybody involved. His relationship with his operatives is a kind of parental one, based on trust – that everyone will fulfil his part and that, should the operation fail, the name of the other participants will be kept secret.

After the fence has the painting, a number of things can happen, depending on how well known the work is, and how faultless was its theft. The machinations are rarely simple. A stolen painting is only semi-negotiable – not like jewels which can be broken down, sold separately, buried, hidden on one's person.

The more hands through which a stolen art object passes, thus obscuring its origin, the more secure its sale becomes.

In some countries, like Switzerland, there are no customs restrictions on the import and export of works of art. And in addition, under Swiss law the buyer of a stolen object which has passed through other hands since its theft is not implicated as a receiver of stolen goods. For these reasons, it is towards Switzerland that much of the world's stolen art makes its way. The story of the *Madonna del Cossito* is a good illustration of how this works.

The picture, a thirteenth century painting on panel, valued at $1 million, was stolen in 1964 from a small church near Rome. It was taken first to Milan, where a restorer made slight changes in its appearance to reduce the possibility of its being recognized, then to Switzerland, where it was listed by the receiving dealer in the catalogue for a little-publicized auction to be held in Liechtenstein. These notorious auctions, held in Berne, Zurich and Liechtenstein, are frequented by a closed group of dealers whose main purpose is to establish credentials for a dubious work, and an alibi for themselves, should the work be stolen. If it is discovered that the painting is stolen or smuggled, the dealer can always say that he bought it innocently, at a public auction; the auctioneer can say that it was just another painting, among hundreds brought to him for sale. The *Madonna del Cossito* was bought by one of the dealers in this circuit, and disappeared for several years.

In 1967, the painting was offered to a New York dealer. Seeing the apparent value of the picture, and deeming it to be of Italian origin, he was suspicious. Italy has rigid export laws for works of art, which are considered national cultural property. The dealer consulted a scholar who speculated that the painting might be the *Madonna del Cossito*. A photograph was obtained and the scholar was able to identify the painting, in spite of its alterations. Meanwhile, the seller was contacted in Punte del Este, Uruguay, where he maintained a residence. He hesitated to negotiate over long distance, and the New York dealer refused to buy the painting without having it looked at by an expert. The seller reluctantly agreed to a rendezvous, which was set at a villa he owned on Lake Lucerne in Switzerland. The 'expert' who was called in for the verification was Rudolfo Siviero, Italy's Plenipotentiary Minister in charge of the Delegation for the Recovery of Works of Art. He seized the painting, and several other stolen works of art which were found there.

The art underground's activities are more widespread than simply stealing and disposing of works of art. Dealers in stolen art are also busy appraising private collections to see what works might be stealable at some future date. Part of the work of the art thief is to slip unnoticed into an apartment or country house and photograph the objects of value. The photographs are circulated until a buyer is found. Then, with the transaction secure, the work is stolen. This practice is common, and it is not unusual for the police to find among the belongings of a criminal arrested on another charge, photographs of many works of art, some stolen and others still hanging on the walls of their unsuspecting owners. A few years ago, when the Italian police raided the Rome apartment of a notorious American dealer, they found no stolen objects, but did seize hundreds of photos of antiquities alleged to have come from illicit excavations.

Linked to such operations is the legendary millionaire collector, with his clandestine museum. Although the police in most countries pointedly deny that the theft of masterpieces ever has to do with so romantic an individual, the files of Interpol do contain the name of one such collector, an American millionaire. He is said to have fled from California in 1961, when he was suspected of having organized the theft of several paintings, valued together at $780,000. His name next appeared as a suspect for the theft of the Goya *Duke of Wellington*, and he was said to have been involved in thefts in Italy and Sicily. He was also suspected by the FBI of being the 'brains' of an international art theft ring. But when Interpol asked whether he had in fact been involved in thefts in Italy, the Italian police replied that they had never heard of him. And although he certainly had nothing to do with the disappearance of the *Duke of Wellington* his involvement in other thefts has neither been corroborated nor disproved.

Many legal technicalities and private services can be used to facilitate the task of the art thief. One is the 'statute of limitations', which allows for a periodic legal house-cleaning by providing that, after a lapse of time, a criminal can no longer be punished for a given crime. In the case of thefts, from three to ten years after the theft (depending on the country), the person in possession of stolen material can no longer be charged with stealing the merchandise; and in most countries, after thirty years, the owner of the stolen property loses his claim of ownership.

In its simplest application to art theft, the statute of limitations works like this. A painting is stolen and the dealer puts it away in a bank vault until the period has expired (five years in France, seven in England and the U.S.A., ten years in Italy). At the end of that time, he contacts the owner and offers to sell the work back to him. He proposes that they split the going market value – i.e. that the owner pay fifty per cent of the painting's value for its return (at least three times what the stolen object would be worth on the black market). If the owner wants the painting back, he has no recourse but to comply. With the statutory period expired, there is no prosecutable crime, and the police will probably not be interested in simply helping the owner get his painting back. If the owner does not wish to cooperate, the dealer is still in a much improved position. From Switzerland, where he may have stored the painting, he can offer it openly, with no fear of prosecution, and little fear that the Swiss police would decide to seize merchandise stolen in another country without a specific demand from that country to do so. The value of the painting has probably appreciated, and, if it is not too well known, he can hope to negotiate it on the open market, thus realizing its full value, rather than a fraction.

The bank vault is an important element in this process. It has often been asked, but not satisfactorily answered, why banks do not require some proof of ownership when they accept paintings for storage, or screen the merchandise they house in their vaults. There have been several cases where, once a criminal was arrested, the stolen objects were mysteriously produced by a bank. A dealer in old master paintings in Chiasso, Switzerland, was robbed of eleven paintings, valued at over 2 million Swiss francs ($500,000), and the police eventually recovered some of these paintings from a bank in Lausanne. A dealer in England was sentenced for dealing in stolen art, and some paintings were returned to the police by another Swiss bank. By and large, though, it would seem that the anonymity that protects every private person who puts something in a safety deposit vault, also protects the art thief.

Banks have even been known to play a more active role in questionable art transactions. A dealer in Geneva, for example, recently bought a small Caravaggio that was offered to him by a representative of a Swiss bank. Having bought it, he discovered that it had last been owned by a Florentine family, and a little more research revealed that the painting had disappeared from that collection during the 1940s. It being already more than thirty years later, he realized that all Italian legal claims on the painting would have expired. The Caravaggio was legally his.

The dealer nevertheless went to the Italian authorities, with whom he was anxious to keep on good terms, and offered to sell them the Caravaggio for the same price ($250,000) he had paid for it. The Italian government could not raise the money, and the dealer kept the painting. Given the circumstances and the peculiarities of the law, one cannot blame him for doing so.

Another device used by the dealer in stolen art is that of replacing the original work with a copy, unnoticed by the owner. Every once in a while even a museum experiences this. In November 1972, the Cooper-Hewitt Museum in New York opened an exhibition of old master prints. In January, a scholar visiting the exhibition looked at the Rembrandt etching *St Jerome Reading in an Italian Landscape* and exclaimed in horror, 'My God, what's that?' 'That' turned out to be an illustration of the etching torn from the exhibition catalogue. Another visitor had taken the picture off the wall, removed it from its frame, and replaced it with the reproduction which he then hung in its place. The FBI was called in but their expert drily assured the museum's director that 'anybody sophisticated enough to carry off that theft would have no trouble reselling the work in Europe.' Luck, however, was with the museum; the print was later returned anonymously to the museum by mail.

The ingenuity and tenacity of professional art thieves are often impressive. A thief in Poitiers broke into the cathedral on fifteen successive nights just to steal the Bohemian glass prisms from the chandeliers, which he was methodically replacing with plastic ones bought from a hardware store. Scotland Yard's art squad told me of one dealer who stole paintings in the United States and tried to sell them in Canada; then he turned up in London offering rare books stolen from the New York Public Library, but he had disappeared from England before he could be caught. His next move was to buy a château in Switzerland, which contained a famous collection of antique firearms – both the château and the collection classified as national monuments. Scotland Yard had been tipped off that he intended to replace the guns with fakes and sell the originals. Police and dealers throughout Europe who had been warned of the fraud were waiting, with a certain relish, for the first of the guns to turn up on the market.

It is perhaps comforting to know that these sales happen most often within a closed milieu and rarely involve an innocent buyer. But there are some which depend upon the existence of a dupe. A famous European example of this is the château sale. A relatively uninformed but wealthy-looking tourist, poking through antique and *brocante* shops in the hope of finding a good buy, will be offered a chance to see some works of art under 'speci... conditions'. An aristocratic family in need of money has decided to part with a few fine objects. The buyer goes to see the works in a lovely but run-down château. The paintings are priced very low. He wonders why. The owner, he is told, must sell rapidly, and without attracting publicity. One of the conditions of the sale is that the seller and exact price will be undisclosed in the bill of sale. The collector buys, departs, and receives the paintings, which he keeps, respecting the conditions of the sale, for some time. It is only perhaps in reselling the works that it may be discovered that they were stolen – transported for the sale to the château, which the dealer had rented in order to provide the proper ambiance to quiet the buyer's doubts. There are enough fine but unidentifiable paintings – works by such painters as Greuze, Bonnard, Boudin, Pissarro (all notorious theft targets) – to keep the racket going for many years. The one thing the buyer never seems to learn is that, on the contemporary art market there is always a reason for a work of art being underpriced. A common reason is that it is stolen.

The dupe is not always an uninformed man off the street, for the daring of some black market dealers can be flabbergasting. In 1971, when the newly-installed Findlay Gallery held its first exhibition in Paris, the event was clouded by the discovery that one of the paintings in the exhibition, the Salvador Dali *La Femme à la Tête de Rose*, had been stolen from a gallery in Zurich in 1968. The police informed the Findlay Gallery manager of this fact, and she was puzzled, for the painting had been loaned to the exhibition by Dali himself.

Dali was contacted and the amazing story was unravelled. He had recently been approached, as he sat in the lobby of the Hotel Crillon in Paris, by a man who asked him to authenticate a painting. It was *La Femme à la Tête de Rose*. Dali was excited to see the picture. He had been extremely fond of it when he painted it, but had lost track of where the painting had gone since. He offered to buy it, and the man agreed to sell. Dali wrote a cheque, and the man departed, doubtless well pleased to have obtained a fine sum for the painting, and from the artist himself, who had no suspicion that it could be stolen.

Black market vendors are often even successful in selling stolen works of art to other dealers who have no idea of their origin. Such dealers express righteous indignation over art theft – and over being associated with it by implication. They suffer, they will tell you, more than anybody else. The black market, they say, casts an unjustified shadow over all art dealers.

If this is true, it is partly due to the fact that most dealers are less cooperative than they could be over making public what they know about the black market. Perhaps because of the peculiar moral code that exists in the profession, dealers are often hesitant to press charges against a vendor of stolen merchandise, if he is also a dealer. One dealer in Asian antiquities told me that he was offered, in Bangkok, a famous monumental work of Khmer art which he knew to be stolen from the national museum in Phnom-Penh. What did he do, I asked. 'Of course I tried to buy it,' he said. I couldn't hide my amazement, and he went on to say, 'Oh, I would have turned it over to the Chairman of the Commission on Monuments and Fine Arts in South-east Asia for safe keeping until it could go back to Phnom-Penh.' I asked him what had happened. 'The police seized it before the deal could go through.'

When I suggested that he could perhaps have told the police himself, he replied, 'Oh, but I'd known this dealer for years. And besides, if I had given it up, it would have just ended up in the hands of some crooked official and been sold again. They're all corrupt.'

New York art squad detective Robert Volpe told me that private dealers often know, when a painting is stolen from them, in whose hands it will probably be. They want the police to get it back, and the matter to be dropped afterwards. For better or worse, this is the peculiar morality of the profession. ('Doctors do the same thing,' one dealer said with a shrug.) And suspicion or concrete knowledge that a 'hot' work is on the market rarely reaches the ears of the authorities. Dealers have their own ways of checking and prefer their own means of verification to those of the police. These means are indeed very effective, but too often dealers will not bother to take the time. Some fine Chinese objects were stolen from a New York dealer, and shortly afterwards turned up in the window of another gallery around the corner. The latter had bought them from a young girl in a mink jacket who said she inherited them from her grandmother. It all seemed to fit. But the girl turned out to be a member of a large Brooklyn-based art theft gang, and the objects stolen.

Wasn't there any blame on the part of the person who bought so unquestioningly? I asked the losing dealer. 'He should have asked me,' the dealer reflected. 'The objects had to be mine – in New York they could only have been mine.'

As incidents increase in which dealers are unwittingly sold a stolen work, perhaps they will begin to cooperate more regularly with authorities. But this cooperation will still not help the buyer, who does not have the dealer's sources of information open to him. When buying an object from one dealer, he can hardly ask the opinion of another regarding its origin. For the buyer, it would seem that the only safe way to purchase art is to buy from an established and reputable dealer . . . and hope for the best.

3

A GREAT INTEREST IN LINEN

The Recovery of Stolen Art

In spite of the growing concern over art thefts, and the willingness of many organizations and cultural groups to help, the job of recovering stolen art is still carried out by pretty much the same people as deal with other kinds of theft: insurance investigators and the police. But because stolen art is art, and not mere stolen merchandise, its recovery is particularly problematical, and both the police and the insurance investigators must modify their traditional roles.

The complications which art recovery presents for the police have already been seen in brief. One of their major problems, in addition to those mentioned in Chapter 1, is the time-consuming and costly nature of the investigations required to track down and recover an art object which is being negotiated on the black market. In the recovery of such art, cooperation between the police and a private investigator is sometimes both necessary and desirable. A private investigator operates from a more advantageous position than the police. He is flexible in terms of the law, and is financed by an insurance company which can afford to spend liberally to recover a work of art.

One of the most successful of the private art investigators was a

Frenchman of Russian descent who operated under several aliases, in this case calling himself Serge Magron. It is he who was responsible, among other things, for the recovery of the important Picasso *Tête d'Arlequin* stolen from the Knoedler Gallery in Paris, and of paintings removed from public museums in Marseille and Epinal.

From the first time I met Magron, a small, trim man in his middle forties, with some of the immaculate appearance of an *antiquaire*, it was apparent that he was a man who was accustomed to action rather than words. We had met to discuss our different perspectives on the art theft problem, and Magron unhesitatingly described himself as a 'practitioner', rather than a 'theorist' on what could be done about stolen art. He had learned all he knew from experience, and had come to some of the same conclusions as those who had organized detailed studies, but by a different route. In order to stop art thefts, we both agreed, more emphasis must be placed on prevention of thefts; and the problem of recovery must be attacked systematically – not with the haphazard attention it is given today.

Magron's first interest in the recovery of stolen art came out of his experience as an antique dealer. Dealing in all kinds of old jewellery, furniture, and minor antiques, he had come across more stolen art than he had imagined could possibly be circulating on the market.

'The process is always the same,' he explains. 'Somebody comes into the shop and wants to sell something small. The next time, he buys something. He poses as either a collector or as a small-time broker. After a while you get to know the guy, and you see him around regularly. Once he has won your confidence, he starts selling you stolen things. He waits until he has the confidence of a dealer, and then he goes and robs a church or a small collection that he's had his eye on the whole time. He may even propose the merchandise before he has it – if you're not interested, he doesn't steal it. Half the time there is no way of knowing unless he shows up with something a little too good, or the police come around asking about him. And when they do find something stolen, whose pocket do you think the money to pay for this little caper comes from? The dealer's.

'It enraged me. The small dealers like myself had a terrifically hard time – but there was easy money in dealing in black market *brocante* – that and fakes. And it's so easy, so easy for them. I thought somebody needed to make it hard.'

Magron began his detective work tracing and recovering stolen jewels. 'I had plenty of practical experience in intelligence work during the war. Instead of being in school at fifteen, I was fighting for the Resistance. And here in Paris, I knew all the dealers. So the work was natural for me.'

As he became known as a fine arts investigator, Magron moved to more and more serious cases. At the time that I met him, he was hoping to cap his career with the recovery of the Schongauer *Madonna of the Rosebush*, whose whereabouts he thought he knew. He then planned to retire from the front line, for two reasons: the personal danger was becoming too great, and he felt that the value of his work was nullified by the limited approach taken by his sponsors. He wasn't doing a thing about the *problem*, he complained, and that worried him. He hadn't helped to stop the kinds of dishonest dealing that had compelled him to start the work. He had missed his ideal. Instead, he had solved a few spectacular cases and exposed himself to enormous danger in order to do so.

In spite of his sense of defeated idealism, Magron could not resist sharing with me the triumphs of his career. He showed me photographs of himself, always difficult to recognize in his varying disguises, at café and restaurant rendezvous with different underground art sellers. The photos, taken clandestinely, were invaluable to the police in identifying the dealers, who as often as not were themselves operating under false identities. He told me of the hair-raising experience of hearing himself described as a known detective, in a conversation between two black market dealers – the description slightly askew, making him a little older, larger and heavier than he is. Then he showed me a photograph of himself – suntanned, dressed *à l'Américaine*, wearing a convincing blond wig and Ray Ban sunglasses – walking with another man down the Champs Elysées. In this picture, he told me, he was taking an underground art seller to his bank, to prove to him that he had enough cash to make the connection he was negotiating. The photograph fascinated me. I asked him who the man was.

Magron told me that the gangster (whom I will call Carlo Randazzo) was an Italian Mafioso, very important in the Paris drug ring, who also ran an elegant custom-made shirt shop near the Champs-Elysées. That had been one of Magron's most interesting cases.

In September 1972, eleven important modern paintings had been stolen from a Paris gallery, among them works by Picasso, Vlaminck, Pissarro, Derain, Sisley and Utrillo. The first investigation yielded no trace of the paintings, and the case, like so many others, was put on ice until the moment when a chance tip might put the police on the trail of the objects. This moment came only two months later. An informer employed by the narcotics division of the Paris police reported that Carlo Randazzo, a man whom he had been watching in connection with drug traffic had recently received a shipment of presumably stolen paintings.

Magron was called in by the Ministry of the Interior, for whom the case was complicated by Randazzo's drug connections. The police were divided in their opinion of what should be done. Trapping the gangster in the act of trying to sell the paintings would require long negotiations by a policeman posing as a buyer, and the art squad did not have the personnel or funds for such an operation. As an alternative, they could let the drug squad continue its surveillance, and hope that the paintings would eventually be recovered, if Randazzo was arrested on a drug charge. But the art squad was anxious to see the case pursued. The news of Randazzo's arrest would get around the criminal world and perhaps discourage other professional criminals from fencing stolen art. After a long debate, it was decided that the case could best be handled by a private investigator.

The paintings were fortunately insured by Nordstern, the company which carries the insurance policies for much of the art insured in France. The police recommended that a private investigation be made, and Nordstern agreed to pay the expenses. But although Nordstern had a great deal of confidence in Magron, and exceptionally good working relations with the art squad, the police and the insurance company had necessarily divergent viewpoints. To the police the recovery of one painting would serve, in the end, the same purpose as the recovery of ten. It would put the criminals in jail. The insurance company, on the other hand, was not interested in the law, but in getting the art back as inexpensively as possible. It was Magron's job to reconcile these viewpoints.

His first step was to assume a new identity: that of a private art dealer. He went out and bought the wig and American-style clothes I had seen in the picture, then falsified his identification cards and checked into an appropriate hotel – the Lutetia, located in a chic section of Paris's left bank. Then he decided to go shopping at Carlo Randazzo's store.

Magron's first encounter with Randazzo was not particularly fruitful. Randazzo, a heavy-set man with a disquieting glare in his eyes, was indifferent to Magron's attempts at pleasant chatter and did not even pick up a reference Magron made to a common friend. Magron ordered half a dozen monogrammed shirts and left, in any case pleased that his disguise seemed to work.

Afterwards Magron could not resist going to the office of police commissioner Jacques-Paul Mathieu, to show off the disguise. 'But this is ridiculous,' Mathieu said incredulously. 'This is straight out of James Bond!' Although they joked together about Magron's transfiguration, Mathieu was not happy with the cloak and dagger approach. It was Magron's first confrontation with a man of Randazzo's underworld stature, and his donning an incognito would only increase his personal danger if anything should go wrong. Mathieu was also pessimistic when he heard the details of Magron's first encounter with Randazzo. 'Poor man, all you're going to end up with is a closet full of monogrammed shirts.' (Magron remembers that he was much more concerned at the time that he should not end up *in* a closet full of monogrammed shirts!)

A little time had to lapse before Magron could safely make another appearance at Randazzo's shop. He used the time to make the arrangements necessary with the insurance company to receive enough cash to convince the gangster when the time came that he was seriously in business. Three days after the first encounter, he decided to return to Randazzo's shop. Before going, he made arrangements with M. Raymond Schmit, the French director of Nordstern, to be prepared to receive a call from him, and answer anything Magron might say as if he knew just what Magron was talking about.

At the shirt shop, Magron told Randazzo that he had decided to order some more of his shirts, for a friend in New York. This time, although Randazzo chatted a little with him, Magron acted as if he were distracted and pressed for time. While Randazzo was writing the order, Magron abruptly asked to use the phone. He telephoned M. Schmit at Nordstern.

'Mr Dupont?' he spoke quietly, but not so quietly that Randazzo could not overhear. 'S. Magron here. I hope I haven't kept you waiting. I got tied up. Consider the Renoir sold. That's right. In bills, of course. I'll call you later with directions for delivery. And what about the Courbet? You haven't? You will keep me in mind if you decide to let it go? I'm very keen to have it, and my client can offer a good price.'

As he came back to the front of the shop, fumbling in his bulging wallet for money to pay for the shirts, Magron felt Randazzo's eyes on him. After some manoeuvring Magron engaged Randazzo in a conversation about art, telling him that he was art consultant for a number of rich Americans and letting him believe that he was at liberty to buy limited quantities of art for them, but only of top quality. 'Of course, that's the problem,' he said with just a trace of regret in his voice, 'the small number of quality works on the market.' This led into a conversation about the disintegration of life in general. Then, suddenly, Randazzo took the bait:

'I have something that might interest you,' he said tentatively. 'Somebody I know has some paintings he'd let me have to sell on commission.'

'Ah, that's amusing. You trade in shirts and paintings, too. You must have a great interest in linen.'

Randazzo shrugged, put off by Magron's flippancy, and said that Magron would probably not be interested after all. Magron assured him that he would be, provided the paintings were of first quality. He implied that he doubted whether they would be. The conversation became more serious, and after a while Randazzo produced a typewritten list from his wallet. Magron could hardly believe his eyes: the list contained all eleven paintings from the theft.

With no other formalities, Magron's negotiations to buy the paintings began. Randazzo closed his shop, and they adjourned to a bistro to debate prices. As they walked down the street, Magron realized that they were being followed, possibly by drug squad men who were unaware of what was going on. Randazzo was apparently aware of it too, for he suddenly changed his tack and became hostile. Magron managed to get through this difficult moment by feigning insult at Randazzo's accusation that perhaps he was sent by the police. Then he changed the subject to prices, and they were soon deeply involved in an argument over how much would be paid, and how the paintings would be delivered. Randazzo asked Magron to prove his identity, and Magron refused, offering instead to show proof that he could pay for the paintings in cash.

'I'm not worried about that,' Randazzo said, 'I've already seen your wallet.'

Randazzo still seemed suspicious of Magron, but reluctant also to lose the chance of making some easy money. The prospect of the cash apparently convinced him. They went to the restaurant and over lunch decided to make a deal for four paintings; the rest would follow if all went well.

Now that the case was under way, the official tug-of-war peculiar to art recovery began. Mathieu had orders to arrest Randazzo as soon as possible; the police did not want him to escape. Schmit, on the other hand, wanted to recover all the pictures, which would require more negotiations, and a second delivery. But he was reluctant to advance a large sum of money with so little assurance that all the paintings would be returned. If the police arrested Randazzo after the first delivery, the chances of recovering the rest of the works would be reduced; but if they paid for the first delivery and Randazzo skipped out, they would lose all the paintings and a considerable sum of money besides.

In order to buy time and get the money that he needed, Magron assured Schmit that he would be able to bring Mathieu around. In fact he was not so sure, since he knew that Mathieu would be under pressure to make an arrest. By now, getting the paintings back at all costs had become an obsession with Magron. But when he left Schmit's office later that day with a briefcase full of money he was still not completely sure of how he would proceed.

After some delicate negotiations, Magron and Randazzo finally made a rendezvous to see the paintings the following Saturday. But Magron was worried. He knew that something was wrong, but could not put his finger on it. All that week it bothered him and disturbed his sleep. Then on Thursday, while talking with Mathieu, he realized what it was. At their last meeting, just before they parted, Randazzo had casually asked him if he could be reached by phone on Friday morning. It was just a nagging suspicion, a vague premonition, but Magron decided to pay attention to it.

That Friday, Magron rose at 5 a.m., showered, shaved, and, feeling a bit ridiculous, put on his wig and went back to bed. At seven o'clock, he got up again and ordered his breakfast. At 7.30, Randazzo arrived unannounced and Magron's feeling of absurdity changed to relief. He calmly offered Randazzo breakfast, and then they drove in the latter's car to a place near the Porte Maillot. Much to Magron's relief, it was a crowded city street, not an isolated barn or warehouse. They got out of the car and strolled over to the sidewalk terrace of a small restaurant. Magron could not imagine how he could possibly see the paintings there, and said so to Randazzo. The Italian answered that he had the four paintings with him. He was ready to deliver. But then an argument began over the price and the means of delivering the paintings. Randazzo wanted to see the money, but refused to accompany Magron to his bank where the cash was in a safety deposit box. He apparently suspected a trap and would not risk being caught with the paintings in his possession. The argument lasted two hours, the two men sitting alone on the porch of the little bistro with no one else visibly present. In the end, nothing was decided and Randazzo drove Magron back to his hotel. Magron was depressed, realizing that since this first delivery attempt had failed, the possibility of making a deal for all eleven works was also probably gone. He was exhausted and decided to leave Paris for the weekend.

When he returned to the hotel on Sunday night, he phoned Randazzo. Randazzo said that he had come to see Magron on Saturday and that Magron had let him down by leaving town. Now he was full of hesitations. The two men talked at some length, but no new arrangements were made.

Next day Magron found that Schmit was also unhappy. The costly affair was dragging on with no results, and Mathieu was impatient. Exasperated by the turn of events, Magron decided to gamble. He telephoned Randazzo: 'I'm coming by your shop in three-quarters of an hour. We can take your car or a taxi. I have something to show you.' Randazzo agreed.

In a bravura gesture, Magron took Randazzo to his bank – past the double steel gates leading to the safety deposit boxes and inside, to the rows of polished stainless steel vaults. Randazzo sat down at the desk inside the narrow room and Magron proceeded to his box, accompanied by a uniformed guard. A minute later, he came back with his briefcase and put it down on the table in front of Randazzo. The lock turned away from Randazzo, he composed the combination and opened it. In spite of his desire to appear unmoved, Randazzo could not hide his fascination. He fingered the neat stacks of 500-franc notes, then took some out, to assure himself that the same thing was underneath. He was visibly shaken.

Not a word was exchanged as Magron and Randazzo drove back to the shop, but Magron sensed that he had gained the upper hand. As they parted he told Randazzo 'I'm going to Beirut for a few days – phone me on Friday if you're interested in concluding this deal. If not, forget it. I have very little time left.'

After their conversation, Magron telephoned Mathieu's office to tell him that there was still hope, but he was told that Mathieu had left abruptly for Marseille, where a museum had been robbed – Magron would have to work with one of Mathieu's colleagues. Without Mathieu, who had promised to hold off as long as possible, an arrest would be made soon.

On Friday no phone call came, and on Saturday Magron decided that he must play his last card. He phoned Randazzo and was told by his wife that he was ill. He could not come to the phone. Magron told her that he was leaving for the United States very shortly, and that he needed some pictures of Randazzo's shirt styles before he left. When could he see her husband? She said she could give Magron an appointment for the day after tomorrow, Monday. When Magron hung up, it was almost eleven o'clock. He phoned for breakfast, then made some other calls. As he was hanging up the phone, there was a knock at the door. Sure that it was his breakfast, Magron shouted '*Entrez.*' As the door began to open, he jerked on his wig, just for good measure. Randazzo walked in. Magron was stunned – he wasn't even sure his wig was on straight. The idea of another surprise visit and the effect it had had on Magron seemed to please Randazzo enormously. He joked for a few minutes, while Magron, still not able to get a look at himself in a mirror, wondered what Randazzo's jocular manner meant. In the end, Magron seemed to pass the test. His visitor proposed another rendezvous for Monday and Magron agreed.

'Only this time don't show up a day early,' Magron chided. 'The bank is closed on Sunday.'

Randazzo was amused, and left in good humour. Magron phoned the police. Mathieu was still away, so there was nothing to do but arrange for an arrest. He told them to station men at the bank. If Magron put on his sunglasses on arrival, it meant that the paintings were with them, and the police could make their arrest. Magron was also tired by now, and realized that it would have to be some of the paintings or nothing.

On Monday morning, Randazzo arrived as expected, and things went smoothly. He and Magron drove to an isolated farmhouse somewhere in the country south-west of Paris, where the four paintings were hidden in the loft of a barn. Magron checked them and saw that they were authentic and in good condition, and they put them into the car and started back to Paris. On the way, a big black car passed them, then fell behind, stopping a short distance down the road when Randazzo stopped for petrol. At first, Magron thought that it was the police and had a moment's fright. But since Randazzo, who had also noticed them, was not alarmed, Magron realized that the car was his. This was also worrying. Magron had thought that Randazzo was operating alone, and so had the police. If the car stayed with them all the way to the bank, the police would have a tougher time than they were bargaining for, and Magron would have his escape cut off. But as they arrived in Paris, the black car suddenly quit them, and they proceeded to the bank alone.

As they pulled up to the bank, the black car was not in sight, – nor was any policeman Magron recognized. But there was no way to back out now. Magron got out of the car and went into the bank, casually putting on his sunglasses as he walked. From the corner of his eye, he saw three men descending rapidly on Randazzo's car. Magron slipped out a side door of the bank, darted through the busy traffic and disappeared.

For Serge Magron, the case was concluded. Randazzo's accomplice, the man who had stolen the paintings, fled to Spain, but was arrested on his return, and questioning of the two led to the recovery of five more of the paintings. Two are still unrecovered. Randazzo is at present serving a prison term, and ostensibly believes Magron to be wanted by the police. Or perhaps he is secretly out for Magron's blood. There is no way of telling. In any case, there are others who are. This is why Magron has gone underground and renounced his career. For this reason, and also because of the utter futility of the battle he was fighting.

Serge Magron says that much of the art underground in France and Italy consists of gangsters and fences holding paintings that are blocked and unnegotiable, and that slow, consistent efforts and a certain expenditure could draw many of these works from their hiding places. So far, though, he has never been allowed to try this approach. His employers are interested in immediate results. 'The police and the insurance company will never let me buy, and lose the money, in order to establish myself and go after other things [an ironic reversal of the process which he described earlier, by which small-time thieves win a merchant's trust, then pass off stolen objects]. If they want to stop art thefts, those who can pay for the recovery of art must support those who cannot.'

This is perhaps the central problem of art recovery, and Magron's case illustrates it well. He complains that the risks involved in establishing false identities and arranging to buy stolen pictures are run in vain if the middleman, who could put him on the track of other stolen works, is arrested each time; often in the middle of negotiations.

Magron showed me pictures he carried of well-known lost

works of art, whose recovery was not being pursued by the police, and whose owner (often a museum) could not afford to make a private investigation. These he showed to the underworld operators with whom he dealt, hoping to come across a trace. Every time one of Magron's contacts was arrested, these initiatives were lost; and Magron was all the more likely to be known the next time.

To complicate his position further, Magron had no authority to go ahead with an investigation when he stumbled upon information regarding a stolen work of art, unless he was commissioned to do so by the police or by an insurance company. Often the police did not have the money even to meet his expenses, and insurance companies' expenditures are limited only to the works of art that they themselves insure. There is no existing body which will sponsor the recovery of *any* stolen painting, or which deals exclusively with art thefts.

Magron once decided to organize one. The lines along which he planned its operation were simple, the same as had been proposed at all the UNESCO meetings, and probably will be suggested at future ones. The points of attack are: security, inventory, rapid diffusion and exchange of information, inter-governmental and inter-police cooperation, standard certification for export of works of art. Magron hoped to raise enough money from recovery to set up an office as a central point of reference. Works of art would be registered, and information given about specific works and the reliability of the sellers. His office would photograph and issue certificates for works of art, thus making stolen objects easier to identify and much more difficult to negotiate. A special unit would work with museums, to recommend security measures, and another would work with the national inventory. Public collections would be photographed and registered free of charge; the cost would be borne by private collectors, who could also register their collections, at a nominal fee. The police would contribute the use of their computer; there would be special liaison with Interpol to record all the information received there on art thefts. Finally, a large part of the expenses would be paid for by the revenue from art recoveries, in the form of premiums paid by insurance companies and governments. With more investigations, revenues would increase, and Magron's investigators could then afford to investigate cases where the works of art were not insured, and the owner could not pay for their recovery. The office, conceived to serve France, would ideally soon have counterparts throughout Europe. It would be a model for, and cooperate with, other such offices as they developed.

After his office had been operating six months, I called Serge Magron to ask him how business was going.

'Badly,' he answered.

I had already heard this through the grapevine. 'What went wrong?' I asked.

'You know, in France, nothing changes easily,' he said. 'Come and see me, I can't explain on the phone.'

Magron had, in effect, been defeated by officialdom. As a private investigator, he had no right to make arrests. This posed no real problem when he worked in France, where he was in close contact with the police. But often his work would lead him to a rendezvous abroad where his automatic protection was not guaranteed. All depended on the road being cleared ahead of him, and the only proof of his legal activities was an official recommendation. These were slow in coming. In one case, he had been ready to leave for Italy to negotiate the recovery of a collection of old master paintings stolen in Lucca when he learned that the Italian police had issued a warrant for his arrest. As they had not been able to confirm that he was investigating the loss of the paintings, the police had assumed the opposite: that he was trafficking them.

In this case, and others like it, the recovery effort failed because the delicate timing of his operations went awry when the administrative channels through which he was forced to operate bogged down.

After six months of trying to establish a civilian unit to deal with all aspects of the problem of art theft, Magron gave up, concluding that no such effort would succeed unless attached to an official organ of power. And as soon as such a unit became official, the inevitable problems of inefficiency and cross purposes would crop up. Other organizations have had similar experiences.

Within Interpol, the question of whether to continue to diffuse bulletins with a photograph of every stolen art object reported to them is hotly debated. The cost of this service is enormous, and statistics on art thefts do not show that it is justified. One national officer claims that only two paintings have ever been recovered as a direct result of the Interpol bulletins: the Rembrandt and the Van Goyen stolen from the Tours museum. Yet this is the only official listing of art thefts that exists. For it to disappear would be tragic.

A number of other private organizations have developed systems for making a centralized inventory of works of art, which would be very helpful in the case of theft. Among these, the best established is the International Art Registry whose system for identification of a work of art was developed by two Scotland Yard detectives. In the event of a theft, the possibility of recovering a registered object, recorded on such an inventory, increases greatly. Further, the International Art Registry has arrangements with a number of insurance companies, which would offer an advantageous insurance rate for objects registered with the organization; thus insuring a valuable collection would be made more economic. Yet this Registry has remained, to the present, in obscurity, having received the cold shoulder from most museums and professional organizations, who find distasteful the idea that a commercial organization should undertake such a task. Many museums further maintain that, there being no official or generally accepted method for museum inventory, their own system is the only one which can cope with the peculiarities of their own collection. No codified system will do.

If you talk to the man who was Serge Magron about art theft

and recovery today, one of the things he constantly gets back to is the irony that he, working all alone, embodied much of the world's effort to retrieve lost art. If art is such a great public concern – a human resource, as it is said, of inestimable value – why will nobody actively support its protection and recovery? His chagrin is intensified by the fact that he required no financial support, but merely the cooperation of police, museum, church and cultural authorities – a cooperation he could not gain. A similar defeat was faced by ICOM when, having offered UNESCO a chance to develop a standard international export certificate for works of art, UNESCO refused on two different occasions to support or even lend its name to such a certificate, even though ICOM was a UNESCO-affiliated organization. It would seem that although such enterprises are struggling for recognition everywhere, they are often caught in a morass of legal contradictions, financial limitations and general confusion which reduces their efficiency to zero.

Serge Magron's disappearance was predestined. He could not have hoped to continue to operate alone. But until some serious international effort replaces this man, whose best single qualification was his determination, we can only believe what the newspapers tell us: the art theft spiral, like the art price and the cost of living spirals, is out of control.

4

AT THE SHRINE OF ART

Art Theft as a Social Phenomenon

Four days before Christmas in 1970 two small works by Picasso, a watercolour and a drawing, were stolen from an exhibition at the Guggenheim Museum in New York. While the museum staff was in hysteria over what to do (the works, valued at $110,000, were uninsured), they got them back. The two Picassos arrived in the next day's mail, in a brown paper package post-marked Grand Central Station. 'A nice Christmas present,' commented the Director of the museum. The drawing had been ripped in two, probably when it was removed from its frame, but restoration was possible and the two small objects were soon back on the wall. 'Well,' said the Director, incoherent with relief as he held the watercolour upside-down for reporters to see at a press conference given to celebrate the recovery, 'they weren't insured, but at least there was no postage due.' Everyone raised his glass of sherry and toasted the returned reason of the thief.

Surely one of the most bizarre aspects of today's art theft problem is the increase in the number of thefts committed by ordinary citizens, who have no profit motive whatever, and steal an object only to keep it. These thefts not only constitute a major administrative headache for the keepers of art in public places, but seem to challenge the basic premise on which public collections are founded. If making art publicly accessible to everyone is a legitimate goal, then why do art lovers steal?

Everyone reading this book has probably had an unfulfilling experience at a museum. Sentiment usually runs with the art-lover-who-steals. Like the student who in 1953 stole a Rodin bronze sculpture from the Victoria and Albert museum, then brought it back a fortnight later when he'd had sufficient time to 'live with it'. As a member of the public, he had borrowed an object that was publicly owned.

One further sympathizes with at least the motive of the theft which is inspired by the seeming indifference of the institution that houses the art, although such incidents sometimes take a bizarre twist. In 1959, for example, a persevering thief broke into the Museum of Applied Arts in Vienna, scaled a wooden enclosure and a six-foot brick wall, and broke the glass in two successive doors in order to arrive in the Carpet Room and steal three seventeenth century Oriental carpets. The following week the museum's director received this letter:

> Dear Director,
>
> As you will have already noticed, I have on my own initiative today borrowed several carpets from your museum so that I may, for artistic purposes, make copies of them. I should never have been able to have obtained permission for this in a legal way. In about three months I shall have finished copying them.
>
> Precisely on the 1st May the carpets will be returned to you, but only if you do not report the matter to the judiciary authorities and do not make this matter public. Otherwise, I shall be forced to destroy the carpets and it will not be possible to return them. Should you nevertheless report the matter to the police or make the matter known to the public, I shall inform the press, in justification, of the downright criminally thoughtless way in which you

guard valuable objects of art (and in this way invite visitors to the museum to take away the articles on show).

I am, Sir,

Most respectfully yours,

F.

In the end the writer turned out to be a lot less innocent than his letter had led one to believe. All three carpets were sold to dealers – one in Athens, one in Beirut and one in Ankara. When the thief was eventually caught (and the carpets recovered) it turned out that this was his fifth museum theft. He had, in fact, picked up his interest in carpets while serving time at Innsbruck for a previous museum theft. During this detention he had been assigned to work as a weaver at the national tapestry factory.

Today, with the visual arts becoming an ever more potent cultural stimulus, the public has both stronger and more complex motives for stealing art than ever before. Their motivation seems to be composed of a strange mixture of love for art, awe at its financial value, and the resentment that often comes from thwarted efforts to experience art in an intimate context. The theft of the small Picassos from the Guggenheim Museum can serve as a fair example to demonstrate the museum-goer's plight.

Any work of art today, at a moment when every newspaper carries sales notices and collector's guides, can be considered a desirable piece of merchandise. Just as price rises of works of art are chartable, so an object's power to attract can also be calculated. There is for every kind of art what might be called a 'desirability quotient' which shows, at any moment, what people will buy, and is also curiously related to what people steal. Among the several factors which constitute an object's desirability are market appeal, aesthetic appeal, snob appeal, and general availability to the average buyer.

The 'desirability quotient' of a Picasso can be considered to be very high, almost uniquely high, because of a particular combination of factors.

Market appeal: Picasso is among the greatest artists of our time and is also a famous public figure whose activities were followed closely by the press and recorded in great detail by his followers; he is also the artist of our epoch who was perhaps most concerned with marketing his work, maintaining his prices, and creating art for buyers at every level. This means that Picassos are readily available and are avidly bought – to the extent that Picasso is a kind of index for the value of modern art. Museums buy the paintings, wealthy collectors snap up drawings, and modest buyers who have money to spend may have one of his production-line lithographs. Although poorer enthusiasts must settle for posters, Picasso is one artist who reproduces extremely well. And even a 'limited edition' poster, a reproduction of a Picasso, is worth something. A Picasso is an investment combining artistic value, historical significance and an element of the mythology of Picasso, the person. It is felt that if you have a Picasso, you have something of value, even if the work itself is relatively mediocre within his *oeuvre*.

Aesthetic appeal: the great Picassos are museum art *par excellence*, in a way that few of his contemporaries' work is. Just as it is possible to say that a Matisse *odalisque* is most appropriately seen within the comfortable bourgeois milieu that it was created for, and not on the neutral wall of a museum, it is impossible to imagine Picasso's *Guernica* hanging anywhere but in an institution. So much of Picasso's work has an element of manifesto and public statement about it, that it rejects the notion of an intimate setting. It can almost be said that museums of contemporary art – a recent invention – were built to house the phenomenon of art as public statement, epitomized by Picasso.

Snob Appeal: Since great Picassos are museum art, and lesser Picassos are also collected incidentally by institutions, the snob appeal of owning any Picasso is great. Lesser works by Picasso, since they can be considered abbreviated versions of the same principles embodied in the museum pieces, are almost like minor relics of a saint.

Availability: The above factors of course mean that any Picasso will be expensive – often beyond reason. The story is told of Picasso's once being haunted while dining in a restaurant, by a young artist who implored him to help her establish herself. Finally Picasso snatched up his napkin, and signed it impatiently. He gave it to the girl, chiding, 'Don't let it go too cheap.'

The great rise in art prices means today that only museums and the richest collectors are allowed to have the best Picassos. In 1969 the Museum of Modern Art in New York bought Gertrude Stein's wonderful collection of 47 paintings (38 of them early Picassos) for $6 million, a price that would surely have impressed Miss Stein, who built her collection painstakingly, always investing modest sums. In the 1960s, Picassos from the generally mediocre 1960 period sold for between $30,000 and $100,000. Almost all of them were sold to museums, other buyers being effectively driven from the market by the prices. And once in museums, the paintings' value can only rise through the fame they gather from reproductions, through exhibitions and posters which reinforce the artist's reputation and appeal, through the number of people who come to see them, and through the prices paid subsequently (probably by museums) for other Picassos.

A paradox arises. The museum visitor's artistic appreciation has been awakened but, if he decides to collect himself, he discovers that only the museums he visits can afford to acquire what they display. Furthermore, he may discover that display in one way distorts the impact of the art itself. The works may be behind glass and difficult to see, or there may be no chairs to sit on, or perhaps there is too much noise, or the lighting is bad. The physical proximity of great and minor works makes the small but admirable things suffer. In any case, the conditions under which the work is available often seem to occasion some kind of spiritual loss. This loss, the art convert may judge to be unfair. Further, the museum has walls and walls crowded with important paintings. While complaining of shortages of funds and space, it seems to be wallowing in a vulgar excess. Why not take one for oneself?

Every museum has been plagued over the last ten years by amateur thefts. They are the reason for concentrated security guards telling you to stay AWAY from the paintings, and why the Louvre and so many other museums must shut down part of their galleries every day in order to have proper security in the galleries that are open. The works are often stolen during visiting hours, when the museum is full. The target objects are small, handsome, and valuable. The art-lover-who-steals chooses as carefully as if he were making a costly purchase. And, because the stolen object will be kept and not sold on the black market, there is virtually no hope of recovery for the museum, once the work goes out of the door. Unless the culprit becomes conscience-stricken, and sacrifices his loot in return for his untroubled sleep.

The thief's rationalization is that the object in the museum is poorly appreciated and poorly seen. If he steals only one small thing (a miniscule loss to the museum, he calculates) he will realize its value and cherish it in a way that it can never be cherished publicly. He can appease his conscience with the comforting quasi-logic that, since he did not steal for money, he did not really steal.

Many unique objects disappear this way. The tiny but priceless oil on copper nature study by the seventeenth-century artist Jan van Kessel stolen from the Prado in July 1971, according to official reports by a tourist, is probably an example. It was hanging, along with other works in the series, in the corridor leading to the cafeteria. Perhaps the thief assumed it was little wanted if it was hanging there. Or perhaps he just acted impulsively – or compulsively. The temptation was too great. At any rate, there was no other way to acquire such an object. An $8 \times 3\frac{1}{2}''$ picture of a bird by a seventeenth-century artist, it would seem, should be priced within a range that anyone who wanted it could afford. In fact, it appears that a work like the one stolen from the Prado has not come to the salesroom since the Second World War. This, too, can be partly attributed to museums, which helped produce the rarity of many desirable categories of works of art, by buying rapaciously and rarely discarding on the open market. Today, they are reaping an ironic reward.

The issue of a museum's responsibility toward its holdings has been periodically debated ever since the *Mona Lisa* was stolen from the Louvre in 1911. The police proceeded to make an investigation, which turned up no clues, while the press venomously condemned the Louvre for its lax security. One of the foremost critics in the press, was the poet and critic Guillaume Apollinaire. Shortly after one of his diatribes appeared, the police shocked everybody by arresting Apollinaire as a suspect for the theft of the *Mona Lisa*.

Apollinaire had lived, during his impecunious days, with an extravagant character named Géry Pieret, who had served briefly as his secretary. One afternoon in 1907, upon departing for the Louvre, Pieret had said to Marie Laurencin, Apollinaire's mistress; 'I'm going to the Louvre – can I bring you anything?' She didn't take him seriously, but when he returned, he had in his pockets two Iberian heads, stolen from the ancient sculpture galleries. He sold them to another acquaintance, the young painter Pablo Picasso.

A few years later Pieret was short of cash and decided to visit the Louvre again. This time he took a largish Phoenician statue. Apollinaire and Picasso urged him to return it, and considered returning the heads as well. But while they were arguing about the best course of action, the *Mona Lisa* was stolen, creating an enormous scandal.

Several Paris newspapers patriotically offered a reward for the return of the painting, which prompted Pieret to write to *Paris-Journal*, saying that he knew nothing about the *Mona Lisa*, but proposing that they offer *him*, too, a reward, for the return of the Phoenician statue. Then, to Apollinaire and Picasso's horror, he revealed the whole story of his misdeeds, sold the statue to *Paris-Journal* and fled the country. In his absence, the police seized the next best person – his friend Apollinaire. Apollinaire and Picasso had in the meantime turned over the other stolen goods to *Paris-Journal*, for anonymous restitution. The newspaper used the statues to taunt the Louvre officials for letting the theft happen. Eventually the Director of French Museums was dismissed and the head curator, under heavy criticism, also resigned. A debacle followed the arrest of Apollinaire, who was put in solitary confinement and held and interrogated for six days, then brought to a hearing where Picasso officially denied having anything to do with the affair, and even denied being an acquaintance of Apollinaire. Apollinaire was eventually released, much disillusioned.

Over the years, as threats have increased, the position of the museum administration has become more strictly limited. Louvre curator Germain Bazin, in his book *The Museum Age* recently assumed the ultimate position, suggesting that museums may eventually have to turn away visitors from their best art, and function like libraries where only connoisseurs can see the original 'documents' and plebians would have to be enlightened through reproductions. Although it seems unlikely that our best museums would ever adopt such a gloomy practice, the museum experience is becoming daily a less fulfilling one for visitors, partly because the increase in acts of violence against works of art has led ineluctably to tighter security; and tighter security limits satisfactory contact with art.

If this fact leads visitors to steal in desperation, it also leads many to seek an alternative way and place for appreciating art. One major substitute has been visiting churches. But here, too, the incidence of art visitors has carried in its wake a grave problem of theft.

For several decades there has been a growing awareness of the fact that our museums have become churches, and our churches, museums – a statement which applies in a literal as well as metaphorical sense. The church visitor today is less likely to be a worshipper than a member of the art cult. The art-loving public has joyously discovered the church – lovelier, more comprehensible, more inspiring than the impoverished and dusty local museum – and developed the habit of visiting churches, to the extent that by now the most modest chapel is an automatic stop in any village, whereas the average tourist will shun the small museum that the village may also maintain.

The church began tolerating its secular callers on the theory that visitors, whatever their motive for coming, were better than no visitors. But occasional scholars and art-lovers soon became busloads of organized tourists, and churches were the stopping points around which these tours were organized. There followed a moment of resistance against the seemingly indecent misuse of the place of worship implied by droves of gawking, underdressed visitors, and the church made an effort to maintain a reasonable equilibrium. At St Peter's women with uncovered heads and shoulders and men in shorts were turned away. Italian churchmen balked in horror at mini-skirted culture-seekers, and withered old crones dressed in black appointed themselves the guardians of the faith, keeping stern watch over the sacred portals, castigating the fashionably dressed, cosmopolitan visitors who tried to enter.

But the staunch resistance could not last long, and when the Church's official policy relaxed, the change seemingly swept away all restrictions on the places of worship. The Church's position now has swung to the opposite extreme. There are no prohibitions against gangs of visitors, with shouting guides, and the most austere and out-of-the-way churches have themselves indulged in polyglot squawk boxes to explain the art cycles: '*Que savons-nous de la vie de l'artisan au Moyen-age?*' and boxes where a coin buys neither an intercession nor a meal for the poor, but a two-minute spotlight aimed at a star painting. Church entertainment ranges from *son et lumière* to rock concerts. Tourism, in short, has been a boon to the clergy as religion has faded. It is, in many churches, the parish's most important commodity.

With the influx of visitors, the church has, however, encountered a series of problems that it had never considered before. It began to become apparent that the regard people traditionally had for the place of worship, the very respect for religious art which brought the tours to churches to begin with, had disappeared with the anonymity of the crowds. The rise in the number of church thefts has been dramatic. In Italy alone, religious objects and paintings are disappearing at a rate that more than doubles each year. There, the church has been seen to be the easiest target for the amateur thief, who seeks to steal a great masterpiece and exact a ransom for it, or, if that fails, simply to collect the reward generally offered for giving information leading to the object's recovery. But masterpieces are not the only problem. The number of small objects (candelabra, small pieces of woodwork, etc.) stolen by tourists, as souvenirs, is inestimable.

In a way, this form of art stealing is a little like shoplifting. In 1971 a tourist, it would seem, admired a thirteenth-century panel painting in an isolated church in the Sinai Peninsula, which portrayed one of the Church's founding fathers. On an impulse, he decided to take it along as a souvenir. The painting was, from a financial and a historical point of view, considered priceless – of primary importance. To the tourist, it was no doubt an attractive memento. He very likely slipped it between two folds of a suit, and carried it home in his suitcase. It is unlikely that the painting will ever be recovered.

Part of the problem results from the failure of the old system of faith, from the failure of religion, and the disappearance of a strong respect for authority in general. In the past, even non-believers would have hesitated to steal something from a church, out of superstition or fear (one thinks of some of the tales of the *Decameron*), or simply out of respect for something acknowledged to be sacred. But today church-associated objects are no more and no less than museum objects, and the ambiance in the two places has become strangely interchangeable. A church today is little more than a cooler, quieter, and darker and more poorly-guarded version of a museum. And the treasures in churches are suddenly subject to intensified dangers, since in the inspired ambiance of the church they appear perhaps even more expensive, more beautiful, and more desirable. No physical barrier prevents their being carried off (it is a premise of the church that objects used in worship should be accessible), and moral restraints no longer stop anyone from doing so.

The motivation of some stealers may contain a certain sense of revenge. In Italy, the interest local profiteers have begun to take in their nearby churches seems almost proprietorial – it is not without a certain delectation that one robs the church that played a parental role in one's youth. In the south of Italy, a group of local labourers recently got together and stripped a small twelfth century church of all its frescoes. A message to Interpol registered the murals as stolen, and fixed the date of disappearance as some time within the last twelve years. An unrecognizeable photograph accompanied the report.

The method used to remove the frescoes had been one commonly used by professional restorers, and learned by their assistants: the fresco is painted with glue, a canvas is put over its surface, and when dry the surface is tapped with a rubber hammer. The fresco then adheres to the glued canvas and can be shaved away from the wall to which it is attached. Later it is attached to another surface, and the canvas and soluble glue removed from the front. The process takes some time to accomplish, so evidently the thieves worked at their leisure. Another identical case was next reported near Florence, where an important Renaissance fresco was discovered gone from a village church. The thieves were assumed to have learned the technique for removing it while working on the salvage operation in Florence after the 1966 flood. There are numerous mural pieces exhibited for sale in the galleries and homes of dealers in Switzerland coming from churches in Italy and the villas at Pompeii, which indicate that the process is common.

This is not at all surprising. The decline of faith has caused small churches to close down. The local parish, itself poor enough, cannot afford a guard for what might be a valuable work of art. And, during the indefinite period which passes while the municipality decides what to do with the church, the art disappears. So much art is stolen from poorly guarded and unused churches in Italy that in 1971, when a series of huge paintings by Mattia Preti were stolen from another church in the south, the distinguished Professor Frederico Zeri, an expert on seventeenth-century art, remarked drily that he was not surprised: this was the only thing left south of Naples that was worth stealing.

Tourist shoplifting from churches, on the other hand, seems to be done impulsively, and as thoughtlessly as one might take a towel from a hotel or an ashtray from a restaurant: because it is there, and because it is often neglected, seemingly unimportant to the church where it is kept.

Mrs Dorothy Kraus, the wife of the American art historian Henry Kraus, who recently travelled through Europe with her husband as he studied the construction of the great European cathedrals, related a story to me which indicates how widespread this problem of neglect and disappearance of objects from churches has become. During these travels, Mrs Kraus became interested in small woodwork details found in the choirs of many churches. These details, called misericordes, are richly carved, hinged stools attached to the bottom of the seats of the choir. These seats are usually lowered, so that misericordes are out of sight. They are called misericordes because they were intended for the use of priests who would raise and sit on them surreptitiously during long sermons where they would be required to spend hours standing in one place. The stools, usually bearing grotesque or caricature-like figures meant to be a whimsical commentary on the congregation or perhaps the priest's thoughts, were often carved by the same master who executed the richly ornate stalls and altar.

Mrs Kraus discovered that these decorative pieces had never been catalogued, and that the few photographs of them in the archives of the monuments services of the various countries were unpublished. Many people did not even know of their existence. She decided to write a book about them, and began to record all the misericordes still in existence. One of the first things that struck her was the rapidity with which they were disappearing. In one church, 48 were recorded in 1953, while only 36 remained in 1973. In another, she viewed twenty misericordia in a church, and when she returned a year later, five were gone. In the larger, more important churches, it was often difficult to gain entry to the choir in order to see the stools. In effect, the church had become aware of the problem of theft, and had begun to lock away everything portable.

Sometimes the clergy are simply uninterested in the preservation of artistically valuable things, now that the context of religious usage has disappeared. Mrs Kraus recalls visiting an important church in France and finding several misericordes lying on the floor, having fallen off their hinges and been left there. It is no surprise, in a way, that in the course of time, these neglected objects disappear. Many are not even stolen but are simply put somewhere and forgotten. In addition, with the change to the new liturgy many churches have put away the rich adornments which once were a testimony of the church's power, replaced them with simpler, more modern and 'tasteful' objects, or with nothing at all. Carved choir-stalls, lamps, censers, jewelled reliquaries and ivory crosses are put aside to make room for a clean, simple altar. Very valuable objects are put in museums where, although there is no context for appreciating their function, they are at least safe. Candelabra and richly ornate garments are stored away, and nobody knows exactly when they are first missed. Local antique dealers are anxious to buy such material, and in many cases things are simply sold – sometimes to raise money for the parish, sometimes because priests, too, have not been able to resist the temptation of lining their pockets. There is little chance of the objects being recognized once they have left the church. They can be sold easily on the open market, as antique shops are full of similar crosses, chalices, and chairs, some of which have in the past been legitimately sold by the Church, some by families. Many are fakes or copies made early in this century when the tourist market first opened, which today pass for the real thing.

The solution has been proposed of allowing some sales of unwanted objects, to meet market demand for old religious art, and to rid the church of what is least needed. This, however, is technically illegal in most countries. In France, for example, the law prescribes that the moveable property in churches belongs ultimately to the state, and cannot be sold or transferred. Recently, further measures were passed calling for the immediate inventory of the moveable objects associated with historic monuments and churches, mainly to prevent further sale of church property by priests.

In Belgium, the disappearance of old liturgical objects through theft or unauthorized sale became so accelerated that the government ordered an emergency photographic inventory to be made of all the moveable objects in all the churches of the country, so that none of these objects could circulate on the Belgian art market. This inventory, now near completion, has done much to put the situation in order. In many cases, old photographs were found, showing objects which had been lost to the church as long ago as the Second World War. In some instances, these objects were returned to the churches; in others the photograph aided state restorers in reconstructing woodwork and other features which had been partially destroyed. Again, though, it was often the case that the photographers would arrive to find that the chalice or icon they had come to photograph had disappeared very shortly before their arrival.

Because the situation is at once serious and chaotic, many large churches have reached the conclusion that, for the rest of civilized existence, the art of which they are the guardians, of which they cannot dispose, and which is an important part of their heritage, will have to be kept under lock and key. In more and more cities a pilgrimage to an important church will be futile, since the best art has been removed to a museum. The chapel where the Ghent Altarpiece is kept can be visited only under the watchful eyes of a guardian; the painting itself is protected from too-close scrutiny by a bronze railing, and the crowds deposited by buses are often so great that one can better study the painting by looking at the post cards on the concession that occupies the opposite wall of the room. Gaining access to objects like misericordes will become increasingly difficult for the casual visitor. More and more, the study and appreciation of art have come to rely on photographs. Many of us are so familiar with art through books and slides that seeing the real thing can even be something of a disappointment.

Substitution of near-art for art has a curiously dispiriting effect on people, and intensified security leads many to desperation. To the museum-goer who makes a pilgrimage to the Musée Condé in Chantilly in order to see the *Très Riches Heures du duc de Berry* it is a shock to discover that the manuscript which he stares at across the reflections in the velvet-lined glass-covered case in the rare book room is a facsimile, no different from the one he could see in many libraries, or buy in many bookstores.

I was told a curious story by a worker in a museum in the southern United States. The museum shares its spacious grounds with the residence of the late founder – a huge, mock-Venetian villa, splendid with imported glass, tiles and statues, in the manner of American millionaires' homes in the 1920s. When the museum and mansion first opened to the public in the late 1940s, a young man, neatly dressed, used to come every evening at dusk and prowl about the house – poking into cases and closets which were then still open. Soon he knew everybody.

As the museum's professional staff began to function, install proper security, and label the objects on display, locks were put on the previously unprotected showcases of ancient jewellery, silverware, and valuable things on display in the mansion. Immediately, the lock on the box of Roman and Egyptian scarabs and cameos was broken, and a handful was taken. The young man ceased to appear.

Later he wrote a letter to the ladies who tended the house, thanking them for their hospitality, and confessing the theft. He had learned a lot there, he said, and had come to feel a kind of spiritual kinship with the funny old place. The advent of the locks had changed all that, though, and to regain some of his former pleasure in looking at things, he was compelled to act.

Part 2

THE ANTIQUITIES CRISIS

5

THE REPUTABLE DEALER

Shades of Morality in the Antiquities Business

When the Siva Nataraja of Sivapuram came into the hands of a New York dealer, it caused a resounding uproar in the small world of Asian art connoisseurs. It was the culmination of trouble that had been brewing for almost ten years, among scholars and dealers. In that time, the profession had been stunned by the sudden upsurge in looting of the world's great shrines and temples – the direct result of art profiteering – and it was felt that something had to be done. It was also apparent that any change in the situation would have to be initiated by those who participated in the market. For unlike the problem of art theft, an unexpected and uncontrollable manifestation that threatened the art public and profession alike, the antiquities crisis was a subtle matter, resulting from no more than abusive exploitation of something that had long been an approved market commodity.

The acquisition of this important sculpture by the New York dealer brought two important issues to the fore. The first was over the responsibility of dealers in directly or indirectly encouraging the looting which was taking place – over the ethical position required of a reputable dealer. The second was whether a dealer would continue to be able to dispose of such works.

It had been known for years that the famous Siva had disappeared from the temple in the south Indian state of Madras, where it had been part of the programme of worship. The bronze statue, dated by scholars to the tenth century A.D., represents the Hindu god Siva dancing the world into existence: 'Siva Nataraja,' Lord of Dancers. The great four-armed god, dancing in a ring of cosmic fire, embodies the rhythm that is the source of all life and movement. The gestures of the dance, together with the various objects which the god wears and holds, allude to the five processes by which the existence of the universe is sustained: creation, preservation, destruction, illusion, and salvation. The image of the dancing Siva is one of the most dazzling metaphors in Indian art, and the Siva Nataraja of Sivapuram is a masterpiece among such images.

The Sivapuram Nataraja had been dug up in 1952, along with five other sculptures from the same temple, by a local resident. According to Douglas Barrett, Keeper of Oriental Antiquities at the British Museum, it was one of the earliest bronze Natarajas to have survived[1] – a large and beautiful figure, created during the most vigorous period of Indian bronze art, of great aesthetic quality and religious significance.

The Indian government decided that the statue should be left in the shrine, where it could be worshipped, displayed and used in processions, rather than be sent to the museum of the province, where it would be better protected but less frequented. But since the statue was damaged, it first had to be given to a restorer for treatment.

In 1954, the temple officials gave the Nataraja and five other statues to a restorer named Sthapati. In 1956, they received the statues back. In 1958, when Barrett visited the Siva temple to photograph the bronzes, he was struck by how bright the statues looked under the ritual clothing they normally wear. When he examined them, he understood why. The statues in the temple were modern copies. Sthapati, it appeared, had made casting moulds from the original sculptures, cast copies, and sent the copies back to the temple. Barrett notified the proper authorities and Sthapati was eventually arrested. But the Nataraja was no longer in his possession. It had already begun its long and complicated odyssey.*

When, fifteen years later the Nataraja turned up in New York, it was brought to the attention of the authorities by an odd coincidence. In 1972, the Indian government had sent out a worldwide alert listing four other famous statues as stolen cultural property. ICOM published photographs of the objects in question, and immediately received a response, in the form of a letter from an Indian scholar, addressed jointly to ICOM and the Indian Archaeological Survey. While doing research in New York two years before, the scholar had seen one of the statues, a bronze figure of 'a devotee' from the Sun Temple at Katarmal, in the hands of the New York dealer Ben Heller. The scholar further mentioned that Heller also had the Sivapuram Nataraja: 'In his collection, I also saw the famous Chola bronze "Nataraja" from Sivapuram. . . . I strongly feel that such unique works of art should be brought back to India. . . . I am not averse to the idea of exchange of art objects with other museums, but not objects of the kind such as the Sivapuram Nataraja.'

In calling for the return of the Nataraja to India, this letter expressed a viewpoint that had been reached independently by many scholars and dealers – that certain art works should be protected and preserved *in situ*, regardless of their appeal and saleability. This simple conclusion, although it seems realistic enough, was a radical departure from what had always been thought acceptable in antiquities trading, and what even today is common practice.

In only ten years the whole ethical structure of the antiquities trade had changed.

When Ben Heller bought the Siva Nataraja it had already passed through a number of hands. Shortly after the Nataraja was

* In addition to the Nataraja, two other highly important works from the temple, a Ganesa and a Somaskanda, had also disappeared. Neither has since been traced.

restored, Sthapati had sold it to the firm of Thilakar and Dass, which in turn resold it to Lancelot Dane, a European businessman living in Madras. Dane kept the bronze for a few years, without trying to hide the fact that he had it. He even used a photograph of it as the back cover illustration for a brochure he produced called *A Kaleidoscope to Madras* which was circulated upon the occasion of the Queen's visit to that city in 1959.

In the early 1960s, it became generally known that the Nataraja had come into the collection of Beman Behran, a wealthy dealer-collector in Bombay. Many people – dealers and experts alike – saw it there.* The authorities in India who may have known of its presence there, however, seemed unwilling or unable to recover the statue. Beman Behran, it seems, was too wealthy and important to be embarrassed by civil action to establish that the statue was stolen; and the government perhaps lacked the funds which would have allowed it to expropriate the sculpture for a state collection. Furthermore, some Indian museum professionals were apparently led to believe that Behran would make the statue a gift to the state upon his death – an assumption which evidently reinforced the government's reluctance to act. In the circle of Indian art connoisseurs, it was tacitly assumed that the Nataraja would never leave India; that it was not for sale. It therefore came as a surprise, both to Indian officials and to many dealers in the West, when the first news began to circulate, about 1970, that the statue was in New York. This news was followed by considerable speculation among Asian art connoisseurs about the intention of the Indian government to protest about the loss, and about an American museum's reputed plans to acquire the piece. For the time being, though, neither of these predictions was realized. A kind of inertia seemed to prevail. But as resentment continued to grow in Asia over the increasing rate at which fine art objects were disappearing from their native soil, the presence of this important piece on the market became more and more a focus for

* In his book *Early Chola Bronzes* (Bombay, 1965, p. 32) Barrett mentioned that the Nataraja was in a private collection in Bombay.

everyone's speculations about how the conflict between East and West would be resolved.

The inertia was broken by the Indian government's decision to announce the loss of certain important art works. Following this announcement and the scholar's letter in response, the attention of the Indian government quickly focused on the Nataraja.

Only then were Indian police able to trace the sculpture's movements. It seemed that Ben Heller had visited Behran some time before the latter decided to part with the Nataraja. Behran had sold the sculpture in December 1968 to another Bombay dealer-collector who in turn sold it to an obscure New Dehli curio shop owner named Harman Singh. In rapid succession the sculpture changed hands several times, until at some point it made its way to New York, where Ben Heller bought it.

With the work now in the hands of a New York dealer the question of ownership and recovery became clouded. The dealer could have acquired it in perfectly good faith, and legally, or he could have been implicated in smuggling it out of India. The honesty or complicity of the dealer is a delicate matter, on which the possibility of seizing a work of art rests. In the United States, no laws restrict the import of works of art, except the following: the import is illegal if the importer brought the object into the U.S. knowing that it was stolen, provided that the work is worth more than $5000; or if the importer declared the merchandise to be something other than a work of art. If the importer knowingly brings a stolen or falsely declared work of art into the United States, he is guilty, under American customs law, of transporting contraband.

The Indian government could not find out how Heller had come into possession of the statue. Behran and Singh had since died. Another intermediary, Gopal Singh Nepali, had vanished. The American government was asked to intervene, and question Heller on how the sculpture had left India, and come into his possession. Ben Heller explained that he had had nothing to do with the statue's appearance in the United States. He had been sitting in his office one day, when Singh's representative phoned him from the airport asking if he would be interested in buying the Sivapuram Nataraja. Heller had expressed interest and a rendezvous was arranged to see the sculpture at a midtown warehouse. When he saw it, he bought it. Since there were no grounds for disbelieving Heller's story, the Indian government was informed that the import of the Nataraja could not be considered a violation of United States customs regulations and was advised that any claim of their ownership would have to be pursued through civil action.

When the Indian government declared the Siva Nataraja stolen in 1972, it had already been in Heller's possession for more than three years, and he was certainly not disposed to hand it over. Why, he asked, had they done nothing before this date? The Indian government asked if they could reach a compromise, and be allowed to buy the sculpture back. Heller agreeably replied that he was ready to cooperate with any buyer. 'Anyone can see the statue in my living room,' he is reported to have said. 'Anyone with the money can buy it. The asking price is one million dollars.'

The Indians began to consider bringing civil action to prove that the sculpture, having been dug up on Indian soil, was Indian national property; and that it was, moreover, stolen from the temple where it had been placed by the State. In the meantime, Heller managed to find a buyer. He sold it to the collector whose name has been associated since the early 1960s with spectacular purchases for his marvellous collection, and who has recently begun to amass a fabulous collection of Asian art – Norton Simon.

'Norton Simon has just bought something that is going to cause him trouble,' a leading London dealer and Asian art expert told me in March 1973, and I realized from the conversation which followed that he was talking about the Siva Nataraja. He had been explaining to me the arbitrary but important distinctions that he feels exist between right and wrong in antiquities dealing. Art dealing is a self-declaredly amoral profession, where passing off studio works as originals by the master or inventing a Duchess in a painting's past are all too common. But in the trade, there is an upper crust that, for every work sold, guarantees the two following attributes: authenticity (that the work is indeed what the dealer says it is), and provenance (that the work has indeed been in all the previous collections listed, and that its history as presented is, to the dealer's knowledge, authentic).

In the sale of an antiquity, when the question of national policies also arises, (in almost every country of the world, the government must be given a chance to acquire an important work of art before it can be exported from the country; but almost no country's laws prohibit the *import* or ownership of a work of art which was not legally exported from the country of origin) the reputable dealer's position is less clear-cut but consistent with his other guarantees. He assures the buyer that he will have incontestable (if not uncontested) legal title to the work. He does not guarantee that the work has been exported legally from the country of origin, but he can say that within the country where it is sold, the dealer's ownership is affirmed by law. In the world of art, the buyer often cannot judge for himself, cannot know for certain that he is buying what he thinks he is buying, or that the information he receives on the background of an object is the truth. When he buys from an established reputable dealer, he is paying for the dealer's expertise and for the assurance of an upright transaction.

Most of the objects that supply the antiquities market come from countries too large and too poor to protect the cultural wealth which has come to mean big money in the West. These countries have strict laws protecting the antiquities on their soil, regarding the possession, sale and export of these antiquities; but there is little machinery for applying the laws, and in some cases as little intention of doing so.

In India, the situation is particularly clouded. The law specifies, for example, that objects used in religious observances are under the jurisdiction of the cult, rather than the state. This means that, when a statue is no longer used, it can be legally sold by the temple priests. This process is common. When an old statue becomes worn the priests have a new one cast, and the old one is sold. This is how many of the statues in the West come on the market.

The state does not give blanket permission, however, for the export of such objects. A permit must be obtained. But the system for granting permits is recognized to be among the most inefficient in the Orient – thus giving an excuse for by-passing official channels. The government is afterwards in the untenable position of demanding the return of the sculpture (which was illegally exported from the country), but not being able to claim it as national property (since it still belongs to the Western buyer who smuggled it).

In such a nebulous legal situation, the dealers whose profession it is to sell these antiquities in the West are in the centre of a dispute. How much should and can remain in the country, and what is really the property of the State? In the antiquities business, how far a dealer will stretch his advantages contributes to his reputation. In general, the reputable dealer makes the following distinction: he will not sell an antiquity that is stolen in the country of origin (from an institution, a shrine, or an individual), and he will not sell an antiquity that is looted from a monument. This means essentially that he will not trade in antiquities got, for example, by a local dealer through theft from an unprotected museum, a remote shrine or a private home; and he will not sell pieces taken from ancient temples or ruins. He *will* sell: antiquities discovered under the ground, dug up, found 'accidentally' or resulting from non-authorized digging, regardless of the export laws that prevent these objects from escaping to the West. He will also sell antiquities already in the hands of a collector, or objects which have been on the market for some time, even if such an object has belonged to a known shrine or monument.

Illicit excavations supply a large majority of the antiquities on the market – probably around 60 per cent, although nobody can make a precise estimate, and the percentage varies from country to country. Although the most costly and spectacular objects sold are usually monumental sculptures looted from shrines, the great volume of trade is in recently-dug small metal objects, statues, and ceramics. Such objects bring prices ranging from $25 to the $1 million recently paid by the Metropolitan Museum for a Greek vase.

The responsibility for illicit excavations rests largely with the dealers. Whether they be local entrepreneurs or cultivated proprietors of West End shops, it is they who supply the money that makes the system go round. If the dealers didn't buy, peasants wouldn't dig. How does the reputable dealer justify this?

The story of the discovery in Thailand of a unique archaeological site illustrates the problem. The case, which has come to be known as the Ban Chiang scandal, is a thorn in the side of south-east Asian scholars and archaeologists.

A prehistoric cemetery site was discovered in the mid 1960s at the site of Ban Chiang in north-eastern Thailand, and excavated by Vidhya Intakosai, an archaeologist digging for the National Museum. The site yielded lovely red-on-white painted pottery which was immediately seen to resemble the painted pottery of the fifth millenium B.C. Yang Shao civilization in China. The site also yielded undecorated black pottery, which was thought to be still older – may be among the oldest pottery yet discovered on earth.

The exciting news of the discovery reached Bangkok at a moment of boom, just as Bangkok was replacing Istanbul and Hong Kong as the centre of the Eastern antiquities trade. Soon amateur diggers were plying the area, new sites were turned up, and Ban Chiang ware was leaving Bangkok in the luggage of every Western traveller.

The Thai government, despairing of ever achieving any order in their research of the culture whose products were being turned up, placed an official ban on digging at any of the dozen sites in the two provinces where ancient pottery can be found. People in possession of pottery were to hand it over to the authorities within thirty days of the passing of the ordinance, with no penalty to themselves; after that, it would be seized. Any further unauthorized digging was absolutely prohibited. People finding the pottery accidentally through non-illicit means (it is not impossible for such vases to be turned up during construction work), were to hand it over to the government, and would be paid compensation. The penalty for not turning the pottery in to the nearest museum was set at 2000 baht ($100), or a month to a year of imprisonment.

As the London dealer was showing me through his gallery, commenting with chagrin on the damages done by newcomers to the trade who often lack the scruples and the knowledge of the established professionals, we paused before a showcase. He was citing the example of a lintel from a twelfth century temple in Thailand which had been bought, a few years before, by Avery Brundage. The temple was in a besieged zone, and had been blown up, during a military conflict (although some say that a local dealer dynamited the temple, the war providing only a convenient camouflage for his activities). Soldiers in the area had taken the lintel away, and it was soon smuggled out of the country. The Thai government, when it learned of the loss, had made an enraged protest. Brundage responded that he had been unaware of anything illegal about his purchase of the lintel, and eventually returned it without financial compensation, as a gift to Thailand in his name. There were rumours that the local dealer involved had paid a large bribe to a high official in the Thai government to see that there would be no repercussions. And although the Western dealer who had bought and resold the lintel was presumed to be free of blame, the incident had caused considerable ill feelings, because of the evident significance of the sculpture.

Who was it, I asked the London dealer, who had conducted this transaction?

'It was Ben Heller, wasn't it?' he said with an ironic half-smile.* 'You see, Norton Simon will have to have very good connections in India to keep his Nataraja.'

We stopped our tour and looked at the case before us, full of modest but decorative geometric pottery. I asked him what it was.

'Ban Chiang,' he replied, waiting to see if the name elicited a response.

I asked him if the Thai government was now issuing export permits for Ban Chiang ware. He answered my question indirectly, saying that he bought the pots in the knowledge that Bangkok dealers' shops were full of Ban Chiang ware. The presence of the pots for sale, he felt, could be taken as an indication that the government was not strenuously opposing the sale of the pottery.†

'If the peasant who found this pot brought it to the Museum,' he added, turning one of the pots over in his hand, 'he would have been rewarded with about 600 baht for his labour. Six hundred baht, do you know how much that is in pounds? It's nothing. Nothing.'

The Bangkok dealer, he then went on, did not excavate the objects, and cannot be said to be concealing them from the government, since they are on display in the window of his shop. The objects are bought from him in Bangkok, and arrive in Europe without the Western dealer himself ever having engaged in smuggling. (Another dealer, in New York, had earlier told me there was no reason not to buy Cambodian or Burmese art in Bangkok – since it is not against the law. And if he wants an

* In fact, it was not. It was another New York dealer, Peter Marks.

†The Thai government has since begun to apply this ordinance more vigorously, which they recently demonstrated by arresting an Air France employee in Bangkok, for having acquired some ninety objects from Ban Chiang. He was sentenced to a month in jail.

important Thai piece on sale in Bangkok, it is simple: he buys it in Hong Kong. Most of the important Bangkok dealers have another shop in Hong Kong for this purpose.)

At Ban Chiang, continued illicit digging will inevitably occasion the loss of much scientific evidence which might have helped reconstruct our knowledge of this fascinating culture. But the dealer will argue that exhaustive excavation of all the sites would take a century to complete, after which time all the pottery would be in an institution. Meanwhile aesthetic demand for these objects is immediate, and can be judged to be as legitimate as those of human science.

If the reputable dealer immaculately refuses to become involved, he knows that a less scrupulous rival could simply bribe someone in the government to see that his purchase arrives unmolested. It is government officials, many dealers say, who gain most from the black market, and who oppose legalizing any antiquities sales for this reason.

'I'd say that 60 to 70 per cent of the officials responsible for antiquities in the Orient are corrupt,' another European dealer told me. 'I suppose you know that in Indonesia the assistant director of a museum earned, until recently, less than $100 a month. They don't have the money to change a light bulb. The worst museum in the world is in Java. There are rings on the shelves where objects used to sit. Now they have been sold off.' A dealer's refusal to participate in the illicit market is self-defeating. It will not change the market, and will put him out of business.

And it is not only dealers in the profession who seek a realistic way to deal with the struggle. A high-ranking official of a European museum, who is also a recognized Asian art scholar, expressed the same view:

'These countries cannot expect us to do their policing for them, can they? If they make no effort to protect their art, how can I do so? If there is no legal export, how can I export something legally? The only way to live with the antiquities problem is to be sensible about it. I cannot tell an American millionaire how to spend his money. He wouldn't listen to me. All I can do is be sensible in the way I spend mine.'

In ten years, Asian art collecting has changed from the private passion of a few European connoisseurs whose interest developed through personal contact with the East to a fashionable pursuit linked with the contemporary fascination with occult thought and Oriental life-styles. One great impetus for Western interest in the Orient was a series of loan exhibitions which circulated in Europe and America in the early 1960s, intended to increase the prestige of the Asian countries. The museum collecting stimulated by these exhibitions created a market for fine Asian sculpture which has driven prices up enormously, until today an Indian medieval bronze, still a relatively common object on the market, will bring a price that scarcely any Renaissance or classical sculpture left on the market can fetch. And high enough prices make any object look dazzling. The popularization of antiquities has been a great windfall for reputable dealers, but has also left them in a difficult position. Fifteen years ago, there was little chance that a single dealer's transactions would significantly deplete the country's cultural reserve. It was not a question of selling the last, or best Siva in India. Today it is not only a question, it is the object of the game. The dealer with some feeling for art and history finds himself in an untenable position.

The reputable dealer also finds that the supply of non-pillaged antiquities on the market is drying up as sales increase, museums begin collecting, and more dealers in the trade intensify competition. And with governments cracking down, it becomes harder and harder to engage in strictly legal transactions. He has almost no alternative but to indulge in dealing that is technically illegal. He himself must decide what he will consider the acceptable limit.

Knowing this, and seeing the destruction of art from close up, scholars have taken to wholesale condemnation of the league of dealers whom they consider uniquely responsible for the pillage.

Former buyers, alarmed, have stopped collecting. What used to be a friendly relationship, where commerce and connoisseurship were inextricably mixed, has turned into a business arrangement where each side fears it is being betrayed. As prices rise, more and more entrepreneurs make their debut in the antiquities trade, adapting its 'customs' to mean that anything that can be got away with is condoned. To a certain extent, the rest of the trade has followed suit.

The respectable dealer decries the destruction of a shrine from which a lovely statue has been taken in order to grace a collector's living room, but every sale which depends on the export of art objects encourages the process by which such shrines are robbed. For every reputable dealer, there is at least one story of an abuse which leads to objects being destroyed, one story which mars his reputation. One is led to the conclusion that under present conditions, responsible antiquities dealing is itself almost an impossibility.

6

FOUR POUNDS OF SUGAR

Who Does the Dirty Work?

A large relief map of Anatolia which could serve as the digger's guide to the archaeological reserve of Turkey is mounted squarely in front of the visitor who walks into the Izmir museum. The territories of the country's ancient inhabitants – the Phrygians, Phoenicians, Lydians, Assyrians – are distinguished with different colour tints. The Phrygians' yellow is darker where sites are concentrated, and mingles with the rose of the neighbouring Lydians, where the cultures mix and are superimposed. Turkey is one great archaeological site, where memories of the ancient world, and of the centuries of peoples that crossed the land, are apparent everywhere. The towns of Western Anatolia still bear the vestiges of their ancient names – Bergama (Pergamon), Efes (Ephesus), Didim (Didyma), Sart (Sardis), Milas (Miletus). At a single site like Ephesus, a great Roman city covers three more ancient sites below it, and miles of marble streets and undiscovered treasures lie buried below the hills that surround it. The Anatolian peninsula has been a kind of melting pot where every group travelling from east to west has lingered, planted colonies, and left vestiges of its wealth – from the earliest prehistory to the opulent reign of the Ottoman Turks, until the nineteenth century, when the country sank into its present state of poverty.

Today the modernity of Ankara and the oriental mystery of Istanbul stand in sharp contrast to the vast rocky provinces, where villages have remained unchanged for centuries, and inter-village warfare is still known to break out – unchanged, too, but for the introduction of the machine gun.

Villages are little stony conglomerates of unvarying colour which huddle away from the sparsely cultivated hillsides. Within the last few years many of the previously untouched parts of Anatolia have been opened by roads, but the automobile is still rarer than the mule or horse-drawn cart. The arrival of Western visitors carrying cameras draws circles of silent, dark-eyed children in their black school smocks. Some of the more enterprising ones have discovered that a handful of poppies gathered for a visitor is worth a couple of lire (an immeasurable fortune to them), but tourist exploitation is still done in good-humoured ignorance of the nature of the visiting beasts.

An occasional grassy knoll of unnatural size and proportions juts up from the hills as one drives along – a burial mound from who knows what ancient civilization. Maybe it has been looted in centuries past, or perhaps it still contains buried treasures. As one nears the Aegean the remains of the cities of ancient Greece can be seen, nestled into the ends of shallow valleys which were at one time navigable inlets that gave access to the sea. The fields are littered with chunks of carved marble stones from the cornices of classical temples. The round fluted drums which once constituted monumental pillars have been used by succeeding civilizations to build and mend the stone fences that line the road.

Given the remoteness of the villages and the long-lasting esteem that Greek and Roman art have enjoyed, it is no wonder that a looting problem of the first magnitude has developed. Looting has been an Anatolian pastime since the beginning of civilization, but in recent decades it has developed into an organized business. Istanbul is its hub, and a spiral revolves outward, embracing traders, middlemen, shopowners, clergy – and, at the extremities, the local peasants. The local peasant lives on and works the land, and intuitively, or through knowledge gained from generations of hunting, he knows where to find the works of art. Yet to portray his situation fairly is most difficult. There is a tendency to generalize and either to over-emphasise his ruthlessness, or to type him as an ignorant and complacent victim of events. The truth eludes such generalizations, and lies within a much more natural and human situation.

'The era of the stupid peasant is over; assuming it really existed,' said Boston Museum curator Cornelius Vermeule. 'Fifteen years ago I could go into any muddy village of the Near East and step backwards in time; today in the tiniest Turkish town you walk into the local merchant's and see tacked to a wall a list of *Auction Prices Current* issued by Sotheby's and Parke-Bernet.'[1] Although this is something of an exaggeration, there has been a certain loss of innocence in the lower echelons of the antiquities business; a deterioration of the old paternalistic relationship which existed in the Middle East until the traders got wind of the enormous profits to be made.

The peasant himself, as Vermeule implies, is not an ignorant hour-labourer. His working methods are sometimes among the most ingenious and sensitive in the business. The irony of the situation is that, with his improved technology and the intensified demand for the products of his labour, the Turkish pot hunter is still controlled from above, and has been able to do little to better his position in relation to the market. He remains its anonymous dupe.

There are today essentially three antiquities markets in Turkey: the local market for modest objects; the tourist market, and the international market in unique objects. Like the ancient civilizations they exploit, they exist next to and on top of each other, interdependent, intermingled. The official attitude toward looting ranges from tolerance to exasperated helplessness. In the cases where it could be stopped, the market operates fairly openly – yet when an important find is made it again and again eludes the officials and the national museums, which are begging for significant material.

While I was in Turkey last year, I toured the archaeological sites of Western Anatolia with a small group of people invited by the government. The first stop was Sardis, a short distance inland from the coast of Turkey, near Izmir. In the sixth century B.C. it was the Lydian capital of the richest of kings – Croesus himself. Today, the remains of the Lydian civilization at Sardis include a ninth century Temple to Artemis, and a tablet bearing a Greek inscription attesting to the existence of what was, appropriately, the world's first bank. The site is dominated by colossal columns, left from a city built in the time of Alexander the Great. In the hills that form a ring around the Temple site, a large Christian cemetery was also found, and a cache of Byzantine silver coins – the only remnants of the end of Sardis, which was destroyed for the last time by Tamerlane around 1400 A.D. The site is excavated during the summer by a resident archaeological team from Harvard and Cornell Universities.

As the guide explained all this, my attention was caught by two shadowy figures flitting between the columns at the edge of the excavation. They were cupping small objects in their extended hands, disappearing and then reappearing, furtively displaying what appeared to be small figurines. I wandered closer to them, hoping to catch a sight of what they had to offer. 'No,' said the site's guard, who had trailed after me – so half-heartedly that I wasn't sure I was being addressed. I advanced a little more, and 'No,' he said again (apparently his only English), looking the other way, as if he were warning anyone who might be listening not to pet a stray dog. Then he wandered away, making no attempt to shoo the boys from among the columns. By now there were five or six of them. 'No,' he said, as another member of our group passed him, coming to join me. Then he walked over and stood on a large stone nearby, looking past us and saying 'no' anytime anyone looked in the direction of the hawkers.

As our group prepared to leave the site, the band of youths

took off at top speed down the road. When we made our next stop, at a nearby reconstruction of a synagogue built during Roman times, we found out why. There they were, waiting for us to arrive. They came up and showed their wares – one had a Hittite horse-head in terra cotta, another a little figurine of a man in bronze, a third coins of the variety that you see in bales at the bazaars. All were the wretchedest kind of fakes. The prices: $2 and $5 for the coins; $15 for the figurines. We wandered away while the government representative who was accompanying us tried to find out where the objects came from. At this moment, the temple guards, who seemed to rotate together from one site to the other, came ambling up, and Sssst! – the boys dispersed into the hillside. Within fifteen seconds they had disappeared. The guard, while doing his duty, had also given them enough time to make a sale, if there was one to be made.

This scene struck me with a certain irony. 'So this is Sardis,' I thought, looking around at the dull grey columns – a site like any number of other stops on the European tourist's cultural itinerary. There is not much to mark it as the heartland of Western Anatolian antiquities exploitation, and the guide's passing allusion to hillside tombs makes no references to the treasures and scandals that Sardis has recently yielded.

Sardis has since antiquity been known as the El Dorado of the ancient world. Under Gyges, Alyattes and Croesus, Lydia became known for its gold, and for the invention of coinage. Herodotus remarked, when he visited there, that Lydia 'scarcely offers any wonders for the historian to describe, except the gold-dust which is washed down from the range of Tmolus.'[1] The river Pactolus, which bore the gold dust in Herodotus' time, is the same that Midas bathed in and turned its sands gold, in mythology.

Gold looting from the citadel of Sardis and the five-mile-long cemetery at Bin Tepe ('Thousand Mounds') has been avidly pursued since antiquity. When the American excavator Hanfmann recently came upon a looter's tunnel leading to King Alyattes' seventh-century B.C. tomb, he found there a Roman vessel, dropped by hazard, indicating that this tomb's looters, too, were ancient.[1]

In recent years, though, Sardis has been the centre of speculations regarding the origin of several caches of classical jewellery. In 1959, the Schmuckmuseum in Pforzheim, Germany acquired a series of gold items, consisting of a wreath with dense foliage, two necklaces, a pair of earrings, a gold finger ring, two bracelets, and remnants of other adornments, including the remnant of a chain with oblong links, decorated with lions' heads in relief. The group was thought to have come from a single burial site, and Lydia was hypothesized as the source because of the mixed Greek and Persian influences seen in the jewellery (which would have dated from the Hellenistic period). In the 1965 catalogue of the Boston 'Greek Gold' exhibition, Herbert Hoffmann named the find the 'Sardis treasure'. By then, however, another Sardis treasure was rumoured to be in existence, the treasure of Croesus himself.

The present official excavation at Sardis began in 1958, and by 1962 the archaeologist Hanfmann's report alludes to 'two Lydian graves . . . opened by illicit diggers during the winter.'[2] In the excavating party's follow-up to the looting, important pottery and three pieces of jewellery were recovered – a silver hawk, an agate pendant on gold wire, and a granulated gold head. Again, in 1966, Hanfmann's report refers to the attack on the Lydian cemetery by nocturnal diggers. 'In the wake of illicit diggers, Lydian chamber tombs of the sixth and fifth century B.C. were excavated at the eastern end of the cemetery. . . . The largest tomb, which consisted of a long corridor and two chambers, was re-used in late Roman times for a mass burial of some 150 individuals.'[3]

The evidence of looters in the Royal Lydian cemetery led to speculations about what had been found, and in the mid-sixties a rumour passed through the trade of a big find – of four important Lydian tombs containing frescoes, vases, and much gold. But the rumour was never confirmed, except for the inferential evidence of the empty tombs at Sardis.

Nothing more was seen or heard until 1970, when a Boston Sunday paper hinted at the acquisition by the Metropolitan Museum in New York of a collection of classical jewellery. The scandal that year over a gold treasure acquired by the Boston Museum had led someone to divulge the fact that the Metropolitan had another, perhaps greater, hoard. In an article explaining and justifying the Boston Museum's acquisition,[1] the journalist who had been tipped off revealed that the Metropolitan had a treasure of over 200 objects in its basement. He further suggested that the Boston Museum, in exhibiting its hoard, was acting more nobly than the Metropolitan, which was keeping its classical treasure a secret. The Metropolitan then put five pieces from the treasure into its closing exhibition of the 1970 season. When the objects were seen, scholars identified them as Lydian. Conjectures were immediately raised about the illicit digging at Sardis several years before. It was not until three more years had passed, however, that the curator of the museum officially admitted the hoard's existence, and revealed where the objects had come from. They had been bought in two lots between 1966 and 1968 from the Madison Avenue dealer Klejman. The museum had paid over a million dollars. Klejman said that he had bought them in two different European cities from a 'trader' who did not know the difference between these objects and the other 'junk' he was peddling.

To date, Turkish demands that action be taken to restore the objects to Turkey have been answered with sneers from the museum staff, and protests from the curator that he should be treated with due respect for having kept the hoard together. (This is an interesting point. It would seem that if the hoard is still together, the dealer who sold it also deserves some credit. It is professionals in museums, however, who generally congratulate themselves on these socially-conscious gestures, and no dealer has yet challenged them on the point.) In Turkey the national museums have been able to obtain little information about the excavation of the 'Croesus treasure', although they summon and question the American archaeologists who excavate in Turkey whenever the scandal resurfaces in the London or New York papers. Few people have been able to see the famous gold hoard in its entirety, although a few more pieces were shown in the December 1973 Gold exhibition at the Metropolitan Museum. The museum cites shortage of space as the reason that the hoard is not on display.

The 'Croesus' gold hoard's disappearance is only one of a series of losses to Turkey of the most important antiquities found on her soil in recent years. The Boston treasure was another, and early in the 1960s the Dumbarton Oaks Museum in Washington acquired a hoard of Byzantine silver objects which were found near Antalya, on the Southern coast of Turkey, all of which were, again, illegally exported. This time, the Antalya Museum managed to recover part of the treasure by arriving ahead of most of the international dealers who came to call at the tiny town of Kumluca as soon as news of the discovery reached them.

Then, early in 1973, a classical statue was uncovered when a highway was being dug in Eastern Anatolia. The statue, a Roman miniature of the Praxiteles statue of Aphrodite, aroused much local excitement, and was arbitrarily valued at 1,500,000 lire ($100,000). It was put in the local museum for safe keeping, but before it could be transferred to a safer place, was stolen, and disappeared from Turkey. A few years before, an audacious theft from the Izmir Museum, where the night guard was lured out of the windowless turtle-shaped structure and killed when he tried bravely to resist the thieves' entry to the museum, deprived this museum of the most valuable objects in its collection – another gold hoard whose value was assessed at $5 million.

Valuable statues and hidden gold are the irresistible lure of what is popularly called 'bootleg archaeology'. But at this level of the business the actual recompense is usually quite small. For most of the peasants who dig for antiquities, their work is just another form of toil, which adds a meagre supplement to their modest incomes. The decision to work at the illegal excavation is not a conscious one. It is a kind of inevitability in their lives.

Selim, for example, is a farmer who works a plot of land just outside a small town in the barren Cappadocean highlands. This region of central Anatolia is famous for its tenth-century Christian churches cut in the steep cliffs west of modern Kayseri, and for the rich Hittite burial grounds and cities that have been found there. Ceramics from the prehistoric and Hittite periods bear the names of nearby towns – Haçilar, Ugurup, Kanesh – in the vicinity where Selim works. The region is in the present-day business and industrial centre of Turkey, and is linked to Ankara, Izmir and Antalya by highways. The Cappadocean churches have become a favourite stop for tourists, and numerous souvenir and jewellery shops have sprung up in the area. There, merchants sell the less impressive products of excavation, clandestinely, to visiting merchants and even to tourists.

Selim digs with a group of people like him, on the outskirts of the town, moving about the rocky hillside in search of ceramics and figurines. The ultimate strike would be the discovery of an entire Hittite burial. Selim is lucky to work in the team organized by Çan (pronounced roughly John), a weaver who has the reputation of being the best digger in the area. He has found, on his own, a number of ceramic jars and terra-cotta figurines in the Haçilar style, which he sold to travelling merchants, and it is said that he can recognize a burial ground by sight, without probes or extensive digging. The sponsor of the dig is the *imam*, the local religious leader, who is given a subsidy for the maintenance of his nearly-abandoned mosque by the agent of an Istanbul antiquities dealer, in return for the first choice of the best products of the excavation, and for news of important discoveries in the area – whether discovered by illicit diggers like Selim's team, or by archaeologists. It is the *imam* who distributes the wages for the excavation work. Payment is made in goods rather than cash, since the *imam* can never guarantee the price the objects will bring from the travelling merchant, or the dealers of Kayseri. For a good find of pots, resulting from several nights of labour, Selim's share will be four pounds of sugar.

It is the early spring, a good digging time since the soil is soft and damp, and the excavations are not difficult to cover. The wind, however, is fierce. Selim's group has been working for several nights planting new pots that the *imam* has supplied them with, because they have heard from Maras, to the south, that a Beirut dealer's runner is in the area. Betting on his inexperience, they are salting their recent digs with broken bronze ornaments, ceramic vessels, censers, and little figurines, which are made in town, and back-filling the holes. When the dealer arrives, they can dig them back out and sell them as antiquities. The agent from Beirut will go to make contact with a merchant in Kayseri and buy, or commission, the goods from him. With the merchant, he will come to the town, and the alderman may bring them to the site. The merchant in Kayseri, himself, does not know the difference between the real objects and the fakes. He sometimes sells antiquities to the Kayseri Museum, and when the museum workers visit his shop, they often tell him that some of the coins or figurines he has are fakes. He generally does not believe them, and saves the objects for a travelling dealer. The price of metal ornaments will be set, at any rate, according to the brut weight value of the metal, so the buyer can hardly lose. The merchant sees no difference between what is old and what is new. He will tell you that the objects are all the same. He will say whatever the buyer wants to hear, and considers it all to be so much madness.

'What is the age of this figurine?'

'Very old, discovered by villagers at Yahyali.'

'Is it Hittite?'

'Hittite style, you see.'

'But is it Hittite?'

'They are all the same, you see. No difference. Hittite style.'

'And this?'

'Very pretty. You like it?'

'No, it is machine-made.'

'Yes, machine-made. You like it?'

About the composition of the object, he will never lie. If a Turk says an ornament is of gold, he is staking his word that it is gold. In this respect, he will be rigorously honest. It is the only standard he has for measuring value – unless, of course, he has a copy of *Auction Prices Current.*

The Kayseri merchant has a private arrangement with the foreman of the team, Çan. He has promised Çan part of his price for any of the best objects coming from the excavation, which Çan brings directly to him, rather than turning over to the *imam.* With Selim and the others the merchant also has secret agreements to pay fifty per cent of the going price of the brut metal for any gold or bronze jewellery that they turn up and bring to him. Thus each of the workers is able to earn some pocket money from the part of the dig which he himself finds. Moreover, when a really important piece is turned up, the team's bargaining power increases.

Such a discovery must be kept a dead secret. Although all the peasants in the town will eventually know, they will respect the secret until the finders have had time to negotiate the object. They may decide to wait for the dealer's agent from Istanbul or Ankara, who, when he visits the towns, goes not only to the alderman or merchant with whom he deals, but also up the remotest goat trails to villages without roads, seeking out the diggers individually, to buy the best of what they have put aside. He pays well. For a Roman ring he may pay $50; a rare Bronze Age pot may be worth $250; or he may trade them quantities of the goods that he is ostensibly peddling – manufactured goods from the city, light machinery, fabrics, grain.

The travelling agents often bring trouble. They encourage the workers to use dynamite to blast away a promising rock-choked site, rather than use their patient digging techniques. The explosions, the talk of discoveries and the subsequent proliferation of outsiders in the region, brings down suspicion from the local museum officials and jealousy from other diggers in the region, who may themselves inform the museum, out of spite. Through this kind of information, the Kayseri Museum managed to uncover thirty illicit sites in their neighbourhood in 1971, which they claimed and excavated officially, by scientific archaeology; and to intercept eighteen transactions, thus recovering important antiquities. The Museum buys regularly from merchants, both in the cities, and in Kayseri: 650 out of the 1000 antiquities acquired by the Kayseri Museum in 1971 were purchased from merchants, 150 from merchants in Kayseri. In spite of the fact that the Museum indirectly supports their work, by occasionally buying products of illicit excavations, the workers never bring their finds to the local museums. Although most of the museums in Turkey have increased their budgets for buying 'fortuitous finds' from local residents, and have tried to cultivate the faith of the illicit finders, they have had little success in convincing the peasants that they can receive a good price for the antiquities they find by bringing them to the museum. The alderman and the travelling dealer are more eloquent.

If the local intermediary is used, competition becomes more intense. He immediately tells his important contact in the city (of which there are, of course, more than one), and if the find is too valuable for them, they inform the international dealers for whom they serve as contacts (again, there may be several). If the find is important enough it may bring dealers from far off places – Basle, Beirut, Ankara, Istanbul, Kabul, Cairo, New York. Generally, though, one dealer has better information than the rest. He arrives or sends his agent with money to buy the antiquities, and money to advance for more digging. The treasure disappears, like a magician's rabbit, in a single flourish. The story is told, for example, of a New York dealer, informed by an Istanbul contact of the possibility of buying a treasure concealed in a tomb near Ephesus. He tied up his yacht at the quayside of Izmir and was taken by night to the isolated tomb. There he looked over the Roman gold, bronze and glass objects, and paid $4000 for them on sight. He returned to his boat and was gone from Turkey by dawn. Turkish museums list some 10,000 objects of unique quality that have evaded them in this way.

For peasants, it is the El Dorado they have been digging for – what has been a $10-$20 labour can suddenly pay them $600 – enough to set up a shop, get ahead of the system. The $4000 from the purchase is distributed through the community, beginning with the Istanbul contact and working down to the local sponsor of the excavation, the owner of the land, the transporter-intermediary, the local police who come in for a cut, and eventually to the workers themselves. Illicit archaeology can justifiably be called a legitimate source of financial relief in the underdeveloped countries. It brings an influx of solid foreign currency; it may support as much as one per cent of the labour force – and an even larger percentage of the total population. Rags to riches stories are widespread, which give illicit archaeology a legendary appeal. In Cyprus, a modern hotel is said to have been built with the proceeds of a single gold hoard. In Costa Rica, a provincial landowner 'impressed everyone by flying to Switzerland with the pieces that he had amassed over a year [as his royalty for allowing the villagers to dig on his land] and bringing back goods and a change in life style that make his boast of a $47,000 sale seem wholly credible.'[1] In the same country three men made $12,400 in a single day,and $13,800 in the next four weeks on a strike of pre-Columbian gold jewellery.[2]

Moreover, a kind of grassroots technique, worthy of consideration by scientific workers, has been discovered by the peasants who dig. Çan, the foreman of Selim's team, is the town's foremost digger. He gained his knowledge of archaeology as a hired digger on a nearby official site. He learned from his work there how to make soundings, and to use steel rods to probe. He can determine the direction and layout of tombs and houses, knows where whole vases and urns are likely to lie, and how to remove ceramics without damaging them. Through silent watchfulness, he has learned a number of things that have never been put into words by the archaeologists themselves.

First there is the question of the recognition of tombs. Çan claims that he does not need the help of the steel rods that some of the diggers use – driving them deep into the ground to feel for the empty space, or the solid roof of a tomb. He also scoffs at the idea of the sophisticated mechanical devices – including periscopes, cameras, strobes, infra-red and aerial photographs, and metal detectors used by some archaeologists, and by the European-sponsored illicit diggers. Çan says he can recognize a tomb by the way the grass grows over it, by the lie of the land, and of course by his knowledge of previous finds.

When it comes to burials in which objects are littered rather than contained within a walled chamber, Çan can tell where and in what direction other pots lie, once he has found one of them. This allows him to dig directly down to the objects in a burial rather than razing the site (and gives the bomb-crater result which is the horror of archaeologists). Once the burial spot is established, or the altar of a shrine, he looks for gold outside it, not within. So the lore goes on, elaborated far beyond what anyone but these workers can imagine.

The pre-Columbian anthropologist Dwight B. Heath recorded similar beliefs in Costa Rica:

> 'They have also elaborated a corpus of theories about Costa Rican archaeology, hypotheses which no archaeologist today can confirm or refute for lack of scientific studies. It is a shame that no archaeologist has yet had the interest to learn what the *huaqueros* [roughly, *pot-hunters*] know. The few reports submitted to the National Museum are too superficial, although one cannot blame the *huaqueros* for the simple reason that no one there has shown interest in such data as are necessary for the reconstruction of prehistory. Among their pragmatic hypotheses are the following: all those who participated in the gold rush at "La Vaca" agree that "*las machas*" were the richest tombs, that is, that there was a special layer of white sand, about eighteen inches below the surface,

> which marked each of the richest burials. They also say that, where there is a stone altar, there is good gold below it. In the Linea Vieja region, some say that neither jade nor gold is found within the stone-lined tombs, but rather outside of them. The neck of a large jar, according to many, points in the direction of other fine large jars. There is a belief that the cemeteries with ceramic of the Huetar style are surrounded by a thick layer of volcanic ash, and that those burials richest in Corobici ceramic are not in the centre of a cemetery but rather outside "the entry" or "the exit" (as they denote the eastern and western extremes). Another hypothesis is that the tiger-shaped metate always has gold upon it; and there are many more such.'[1]

The 'bootleg archaeologist' is a kind of nineteenth-century-style practitioner of what has since become a scientific endeavour. He undergoes all sorts of misery (nights exposed to adverse weather, poor pay, round-the-clock labour), and dangers (internecine competition, danger of discovery, and the possibility of tombs collapsing). In return he has the hope of some day making a big strike, pride in the quality of his work, and a certain gratification from the ultimate destination of the objects he finds. Many workers speak proudly of their finds being in the National Museum, the collection of the American ambassador, or up for sale at Sotheby's – through the same grapevine that carries news of their discoveries they find out these things, and take active interest in them. They are engaged, sometimes innocently, sometimes calculatingly, but with a disarming simplicity, in spreading the antiquities of Turkey haphazardly over the earth. It is a process that, as long as the market exists, will never be brought completely under control. The director of the Çanakkale Museum remarks with chagrin, 'The villagers sell very cheaply whatever they find with the hope of being rich very soon . . . when we confiscate their objects, they continue the commerce more secretly.'[2]

If there is no hub that totally controls the antiquities business, there has been, in the markets of Istanbul and Ankara, a profusion of dealers who function somewhat like a great genie watching over the whole situation, hearing and seeing everything, keeping all fingers busy with diverse meddlings. The dealers of the inner bazaar are to the Turkish antiquities trade as flight controllers are to a large airport. They consider it their responsibility to know the whereabouts not only of the planes destined to land there, but of all the planes taking off, landing in, or passing over the entire region.

The inner bazaar is glittery with the tinsel of brass pots, Turkish coffee grinders, garish carpets, and water pipes. Nothing much distinguishes it from the lively outer bazaar (which specializes in junk) except the darker, cooler, quieter atmosphere. Life seems sluggish and the merchants lean against the door frames of their shops calling out to tourists the virtues of their goods.

The bazaar is not the smuggling hub it once was, partly because foreign publicity has brought tighter application by the government of the law which prohibits the export of all antiquities, and partly because the misdeeds of some craftier-than-usual Turks have given the bazaar the reputation of being rich in fakes. 'The big English dealers don't come here any more,' one stall-owner told me, 'since one of them bought three fakes in Cairo from a Turkish merchant, and paid very dear.' But even without such visits, and under wraps of caution, business goes on as usual.

An unknown buyer there has the constant feeling of watching eyes and of trials to be passed. Requests for antiquities are met with jangly Ottoman earrings and brooches, and small undecorated Roman jugs, which the government makes no effort to control. The outer room of a dealer's shop is crowded with gaudy paraphernalia – bales of coins, guns and swords, icons with silver cases. The same dealer whose inner chamber may contain a heavy walnut desk and glass cases filled with Roman pots, has disorderly piles ranging from coffee grinders to carved Chinese puzzles in his outer room. A chat with a dealer is often interrupted by the abrupt visit of one of the many intermediaries who conduct one around the bazaar, to the final destination: the private appointment at a dealer's home.

At the bazaar in Istanbul, I asked for Roman gold earrings and was taken to a dealer described as 'state-authorized'. He showed me a modest pair of earrings which was displayed in his shop window (with assumed government consent). I asked for something more elaborate, which brought me to another dealer, with a large safe behind him. In showing me numerous cameos and rings, which he pulled from his various pockets, out of his wallet and his shirt, he 'accidentally' unwrapped and began to rewrap a pair of Hellenistic gold earrings. I asked to see them and he shrugged, handing them over – they were lovely, but broken. My usher appeared from nowhere as I walked out of the shop, and guided me determinedly back to the shop where I had started, insisting on the beauty of the Ottoman gold.

'I have already seen what you have,' I said, as he dragged me along to the display case.

'I have many things,' said the voice of the owner from a dark corner, 'that you have not seen.'

The back room was full of dealers and friends gossiping and drinking heavily sweetened tea. We started with a 'do-you-know?' exchange. Then the dealer began to lament the problem of dealing under government control. 'The museum comes here and takes everything I have. They pay me nothing, for what I have bought very dear. Now I have nothing in my shop. Not even a photograph. If someone finds a gold bracelet, the government treats him like me. He gets nothing. And they watch him for the rest of his life.

'Now I am very cautious. I sell to dealers. No museums. They can buy from dealers. I don't export things, you see. But I can recommend someone who does. I know nothing of his business, but I can guarantee it. Of course it will cost more – 10 per cent. But the payment is on delivery. I am honest, but the government is not. It is so easy for them to confiscate things. They take things they don't even want. They think they are punishing me. How am I to stay in business if I cannot serve my clients?' he trailed off.

'But it is safe, completely safe.' He produced a stack of bills of lading as if to testify that the unseen receivers did exist – they bore the names and addresses of art dealers in New York, London, Dusseldorf, the same dealers who will tell you, 'I never import things from Turkey any more; it is impossible. These pieces, I was lucky enough to pick up unidentified at a Paris auction. No one can know the origin of them.'

The conversation drifted to the newspaper scandals of the past years. 'English journalists think such things very important,' he said, referring to the celebrated Dorak treasure affair – in which the British archaeologist James Mellaart encountered a girl wearing a bronze-age bracelet on the train to Izmir, found that she had many more objects like it, and stayed in Izmir two days sketching them at her house. After he published the discovery in the *Illustrated London News*, the Turkish government tried to seize the treasure, and discovered that the gold jewellery, the girl, and the house in Izmir had all disappeared. Mellaart was banned from digging in Turkey, accused of stealing the treasure, and although the British Institute investigated the charge against Mellaart and cleared him, the whole incident has never been cleared up. 'Really, it is all a fraud,' said my friend.

A small man who had been listening silently to our conversation chuckled, his eyes sparkling.

'Not everyone, even in Turkey, knows the story of that,' he said. 'And foreigners are all tied up in knots over it.'

'What is your theory?' I asked the dealer. He shrugged, but looked at his friend, who answered.

'I know the *story*. No theory. The hoard, except for five or six pieces, was made by a friend of mine near Izmir. He makes beautiful fakes.' I thought of a string of fragile ancient gold beads I had seen hanging in an unlikely case full of used watches and old tarnished jewellery in the bazaar at Izmir, and wondered if there was any connection.

I asked him what had happened to the treasure. Had it been sold outside Turkey? And why had it been made? To disgrace the archaeologist Mellaart? To sell it? For amusement? Why?

The storyteller looked at me, smiling calmly, and said nothing. Not defiantly, but secretly – as if to say that the lining of the antiquities business in Turkey was something that he was not about to turn out for a foreigner's inspection.

My host looked at me for a long moment, then said, quietly, 'The prices of my goods range from $400 for a simple Roman ring, to $5000 for a statuette. If you will come back this afternoon, I can arrange for you to see what I have, at the home of a friend.' He sighed, looking tired. Then he added earnestly, 'Although you will be in no danger of harassment, you must understand the importance of telling no one of this rendezvous. Please consider the danger to me. The antiquities law was made by the Ottoman Turks, seventy-five years ago, and today I am expected to live under this repressive regime. The museum wants all the antiquities in Turkey in the name of the Ottoman Turks. I do not believe in the rule of the past. Come this afternoon, if you are interested in buying some beautiful things. But please tell no one.'

As I left his booth, I passed the shop of the dealer with the safe, where the sleight of the hand had shown me the golden earrings. A peasant was there, in baggy farmer's pants, looking humble and hopeful. The shopowner was picking indifferently through the bag full of trinkets and shards the peasant had brought – metal jewellery and embroidered cloths that the peasant had picked from among the worthless old things around his house. The dealer chose a couple of Byzantine crosses and paid the seller with loose money from his pocket.

It occurred to me, as I walked down from the bazaar, that if things are difficult for the dealers, who cannot sell openly something as common as a Roman ring, they are much worse for those whose job it is to unearth those rings, for the proverbial four pounds of sugar. The peasants keep quiet, the dealers complain. But both of them will tell you it is a hard life – that in the end only the middleman makes the real killings.

7
THE PACKAGE DEAL
The Effect of the Middleman in Africa

Both the peasant and the local dealer are stable elements of the illicit market, and their profits are limited by their immobility. Between and around these two fixed points, the middleman moves. It is he who is in the best position to exploit the illicit market – he can buy in the poverty-stricken locale where money is scarce, and sell in the free-spending cities of the world. He is also one of the great beneficiaries of the current strength of the legitimate market. Although he does not actively promote, he benefits from every upward fluctuation of the market; although he does not advertise, he benefits from the publicity given to museums and dealers; and although he does not tout he can only gain from the endless predictions that money invested in art is money well spent. In certain areas of the world, where he can come and go freely without government interference, the middleman has become the local culture's greatest profiteer. Nowhere is this more true than in Africa.

In July 1972, *Business Week* picked entrepreneuring in African art as a winner. A greatest-show-on-earth-style exhibition to promote it was opening at the New York Hilton, the largest African arts and handicrafts exhibition yet to be held in the

United States, and it was expected to burst the market for African ethnographica open at the seams. Native dancers, drummers, films of tribal rituals, African-style punch, and the guest appearance of Zulu King Goodwill were the attractions which drew visitors at $10 a head to the evening buying sessions. The sponsoring company, African Artcraft Pty., Ltd. had some 200,000 objects to sell: jewellery, woven cloths, statues, utensils, and the like – their prices ranging from one dollar for a beaded bracelet to $100,000 for a Bantu chieftain's throne. Back in the hinterland of South Africa, they had 16,000 Bantu workmen mobilized into the craft industry, with another 25,000 in reserve. They were even buying mines for sandstone and, foreseeing the possibility of shortage, timberland for teak. Their avowed hope was to direct a large part of the native population of South Africa into a gigantic art-producing industry.

Since the advent of this new kind of African crafts promotion, which has the potential to suck up the best remaining antiquities together with made-yesterday souvenirs, serious collectors of African art have been shaking their heads and wondering what the consequences of it all will be. They should have started worrying years ago. For although it may be the most spectacular form of African art entrepreneuring yet, this new enterprise is really nothing new. Since the inception of Western taste for the primitive, African art has been collected for the same reasons for which it is now being promoted: it is sophisticated, yet its appeal is primitive; it is a living manifestation of beliefs, and it also fits into a niche of our own aesthetic hierarchy; it is both beautiful and relevant.

Since the 'discovery' of African sculpture by Matisse and Picasso in the first years of this century, its relevance toward a renewal of our vision has been a primary selling point. Primitive art is perhaps unique in the history of collecting in that it was discovered and brought into Western culture as a fully-grown and still living tradition. This fact has had its long- and short-term consequences, its negative and positive aspects. One of the most immediate and noxious side-effects of African art promotion is the extent to which the market has become infiltrated and to some extent controlled by non-connoisseurs, middlemen of the worst sort. They come in all shapes and sizes, white and black. But they seem consistently to follow certain imaginary models, just as real-estate salesmen, car salesmen, and shoe salesmen tend to have prefabricated identities.

For instance, there is a middleman I will call Adubu (or more formally, *Mr* Adubu – the Africans in the trade often go solely by first names). He is a Europeanized Senegalese who wears a double-breasted suit and has a double life style. One for Europe; another, quite different, for West Africa. In Paris, he spends his time basking in the sun and philosophical conversation of the Rhumerie, a boulevard St-Germain café where serious, bearded students pass their afternoons in passionate debate. He occasionally condescends to argue with the students (and also lets them pick up his tabs), playing the role of devil's advocate against African culture. He likes the shock that registers on their faces when he professes disgust for the tribal cultures – nothing, he says, but a remnant from national childhood. The ritual objects – they are amusing, maybe interesting vestiges of a dead world. Like your grandmother's music box. They have no contemporary validity. Nor do the Western-style museums they are boxed up in, in Accra, Lagos, Jos. Nonsense. Life to come lies in the downfall of the West – the vitality of a new Africa, not one that mimes America, not one that fears demons. Neither tribal nor corrupt. Free from decadence, he says serenely, sipping his rum and milk. He drives a white Mercedes and lives in the comfortably bourgeois Madison Hotel.

'Why do I sell African art, the memory of my ancestors?' he says. 'Because it is mine to sell.'

His hotel room is populated with statues which he will dispose of around Europe to the numerous galleries and collectors with whom he trades – big fertile-looking Senufo figurines from Senegal, intricately-detailed Chi Wara masks from Mali, drums and stools from the numerous tribes of Cameroon, little bronze Ashanti figurines from Ghana, even some gold ones, which he will show to a well-heeled prospective buyer if he should hook one in the café. But these wares are of only secondary importance to him. They earn his pocket money. He has carefully hidden away the sculpture that is the real reason for his trip: one of the finest Nigerian bronzes known, the only one to be got out of Nigeria in recent years, the only one on the market; a four-foot high figure, representing a mythical female ancestor – one of seven bronzes that the first king, Tsoede, brought with him when he came by canoe up the Niger River in the sixteenth century and founded the Nupe kingdom. Easily worth $50,000 to any dealer who will buy it. But on that count, he has already had some trouble.

Back in Accra, Adubu has a very different image. He lives as a modest intermediary and local dealer, circulating through Ghana, Nigeria, the Ivory Coast, and his own Senegal to pick up objects from the local agents belonging to the various tribal groups, whom he in turn hires (with his European contacts' money). Much of what he collects he sells locally or in Bamako or Dakar, it not being valuable enough to send to Europe.

Among the African tribes, there is no concept of beauty attached to objects which are made for ritual or functional purposes. The Africans carve jackals and lizards on their pulleys and locks not as a decoration, but as symbols of the gods or mythological events which are associated with the use of the object. In the old days the craftsman created his own designs, in accordance with his understanding of the tribe's beliefs. Now the objects are copied and recopied, former ones put aside when new ones replace them in the same function. There is no value attached to old and new. The objects do, though, have a hierarchic value, because of their *power*, to bring beneficent effects, to conjure strong magic. The most powerful objects are often kept in a special storage house by the tribal chief, and used in important ceremonies – or kept as tribal memories of a great spiritual avatar.

Their forms are copied in new objects, in the hope of reproducing the vital power equation. Traditional forms – the great Baga Nimba masks, the style of Senufo rhythm pounders, Dogon doors – are thus codified.

Coincidentally, or significantly, it is usually the objects with the best magic that we, the African *art* public (the idea of art does not exist *per se* in the vocabulary of the societies that produce the 'art objects') consider to be the most beautiful. These are the ones that dealers and anthropologists have been craftily coaxing away from African tribes since the turn of the century.

For the late-comer like Adubu, this often means that the best prototypes of the tribal style have already been bought by Western museums. From the chieftains, he receives the copies – patinated, hewn, conceived like the others. For reasons he and the chieftains do not understand, but have come to accept, the Western dealers consider these inferior – perhaps they too experience the effects of inferior magic. He sells them to neophytes.

The museum in Accra is his source of information on the value of the traditional objects. He brings things there which he does not recognize, or of which he doubts the authenticity. Sometimes he sells or gives pieces to the museum – it is important to maintain good relations. The museum, for its part, feels the same way. It is surprising to find that the national museums know, and have relations with, most of the major smugglers in their countries. The dealer comes to the museum with almost every valuable object that leaves the country. He wants to be sure of its value, to pick up a free expertise. With an important work, he can be pretty certain that the museum will not be able to afford to buy it, even at an arbitrary below-market cost. For other things – minor objects of more interest to the museum than to a Western collector – he is glad to negotiate with them. It makes for good relations. The museum considers it the lesser of two evils at least to *know* who the middlemen are, and what they are selling. If something of singular importance comes along, they can always try to confiscate it.

Thus, when Adubu came across the bronze of exceptional value, he brought it directly to the museum in Accra. He had picked this statue up from his Nigerian supplier. He knew these fine bronzes were all protected by the national law in Nigeria – called national property, even though they rested legally in the hands of the tribes which have controlled them since the great days of the Ife empire. But once out of Nigeria, there are few legal restraints on such an object.

It had to be stolen, he reasoned, or fake. Although his source insisted he had bought it from the son of the present king of Jebba, Adubu did not accept this story. He nevertheless agreed to take the statue along, promising to pay the finder when he made a sale.

Back in Accra he took it to the museum. From the reaction of the Director, Mr Richard Nunoo, he learned that the statue was real. Nunoo offered to buy it. Adubu made a quick calculation and swallowed hard.

'Seventeen thousand pounds is my price,' he said.

Nunoo expressed keen interest, and promised to have a decision from his board that afternoon (in fact, what he conceived was a trap to recover the statue for Nigeria, if he found out in the meantime that it was what he thought it was). But Adubu was wary. He left the museum with the information he wanted. He saw to it that the statue was carefully hidden (although they could not arrest him for having a Nigerian statue in Ghana, the authorities could try to confiscate it on behalf of the Nigerian government), and then he went to work on his contacts. He sent photographs to dealers in Paris and London. A Belgian dealer he knew passed through town, and he gave him a picture too. The dealer seemed to be enormously excited by the sculpture. Adubu settled down to the pleasant contemplation of the near future with himself a rich man.

In Belgium, nobody had heard anything about a theft of the bronze, and the dealer who received the photograph went straight to the Tervuren Museum to ask the curator what he thought about it. He recounted the story as it was told to him; the sculpture had been sold to a contact of his by the Prince of Jebba.

The curator was surprised. A statue like this – one of the few of its kind actually classified in Nigeria – could not be legally sold, even by its guardian. He warned the dealer that he would have to take action, then the museum informed the Director of Antiquities in Nigeria. It was the first the Director of Antiquities had heard about it.

Only after he had confirmed that it was missing from Nigeria, and cabled this information, could international action be started. Interpol was warned; ICOM passed the information to museum curators in France. The dealer who had been approached traced Adubu to Accra. All that was needed was confirmation that the statue had been stolen, and not secretly sold. This information was slow in coming.

By the time Nigeria knew what Ghana knew, and vice versa, Adubu was sitting in the Rhumerie in Paris, discussing politics. He found that things were more difficult than he had anticipated. Through the French museums, all the dealers knew the sculpture was hot, and the official complaint from Nigeria had got the police on to him. They came and searched his room and seized some statues, although they did not find what they were looking for.

While the police waited, Adubu again disappeared, to another city, hoping to find a collector who would not be so touchy about the source of the sculpture he was buying. In the future, Adubu may well have chided himself, he would avoid talking to that damn museum.

For the typical African dealer in the trade, called by his first name in Paris, Brussels, Marseille, New York, dealing begins with a suitcase full of tribal objects – some good, some worthless – got together by his family, like a bride's dowry to see him through the incidental expenses of his student days abroad. He settles down to peddling beads, wallets and grotesque modern versions of tribal art on the sidewalk, holding back what is better for a profitable sale to a dealer or serious buyer. Connections back home make it easy to arrange his safe exit from the country. (The extended family situation seems to protect everyone. Most of Africa is like Georgia: everybody has a cousin in Congress). And furthermore, he is usually not smuggling. For example, no law in the Ivory Coast protects objects from Ghana; Upper Volta, Gambia, and Togo have no laws at all – and half of what the newly apprenticed dealers bring is merely craft production, 'airport art' made today assembly-line style in most of the poverty-stricken capitals of Africa. The new dealer may eventually develop another trade, preferably one that involves transport or travel as he moves into 'heavy stuff' – real antiquities. Thus one dealer who brings Ivory Coast antiquities to New York, ships refrigerator parts back to his brother. Another is studying the American vegetable canning industry, in order to open a similar factory in his country. Antiquities are a stake in life – the only material thing the African can offer which means something in the currency of the West. They are a ticket to success.

It is through getting to know African culture that many of the European entrepreneur-dealers become involved in antiquities smuggling, as did the Frenchman I will call Marcel Dumur. In 1967, a French Ministry of Culture attaché paid a visit to a museum in Senegal, and found a young fellow-countryman behind a desk, doodling pictures of jets on a yellow legal pad. The main interest in his life, it seemed, was aeroplanes. For his military service, he explained ruefully, he had expressed an interest in aviation and aeronautics, and had been assigned a 'cultural' stint behind the desk of a forgotten African museum. He was counting the days until he could get his life under way.

Two years later our attaché next encountered Dumur, back in France, at the African art course at the Musée de l'Homme, France's foremost ethnographic museum. He looked bright and satisfied. He was working for the airlines, he recounted, flying as a steward, on the Europe-Africa circuit. A furtive smile crossed his face. Africa had got under his skin, he admitted – he couldn't stay away too long from the slow rhythmic pace of life, the different level of consciousness. He had learned a little African philosophy, and even become interested in the art. The night course at the Musée de l'Homme, he explained, was making a connoisseur out of him.

His job in the transportation industry put Dumur in a position that is a smuggler's dream. With contacts in Senegal, and the names of all the dealers who came to the museum, he had little more to do than volunteer for service. He rapidly set up addresses in contact cities, where shipments of exceptionally hot or valuable goods were deposited. He would carry them over, out of the plane, and safely past customs, for a fee. Then as his expertise increased (an ironic by-product of museum art appreciation courses – which breed some of the world's best smugglers), he began to buy and sell on his own, collecting photographs of objects he could not afford, and getting advances from collectors and dealers to procure them. He rapidly set up what can be described as an antiquities prospecting business. It was a simply-organized affair, the same sort of thing that Europeans set up for antiquities exploitation in Latin America.

The principle is simple: first you locate a fruitful and high-quality source of material; then you photograph the objects, and offer European collectors a share in the operation. They advance the capital. Then, with a small plane and a Land-Rover, you go back in and 'extract' the objects. The collectors have the first option of buying, directly and cheaply, art works which on the open market are becoming rare and costly. The prospector can make a nice profit from selling the duplicates. In some countries, his prospecting is legal (in Mali, for example, a licence is purchased which allows a fixed number of objects to be collected in a given district during a limited time). In others, he just ignores the law.

The major problem is to refrain from being too indiscriminate about what to offer to whom. This is how Dumur got into trouble. He carried his open dealing too far. In December 1970, he offered the curator of an important European ethnographic museum a collection of objects stolen from a museum in Nigeria, with the museum's registration labels still on them. The curator was greatly amused by the idea of being offered objects that anybody who could read would know were owned by another museum, and mentioned the incident to a colleague. The colleague passed the information immediately to Nigeria and, after the theft had been verified, Dumur was arrested. Only then did the fact come out that the European museum had actually gone ahead with tentative plans to buy some of the objects. The curator who was offered the pieces had proposed them to the general acquisition committee! Only because a member of the committee, tipped off in advance, asked about the provenance, did the curator admit that the objects bore what he called 'strange markings.' The objects were temporarily withdrawn from consideration, and held for future investigation.

There is still a consensus among too many Westerners that violating the African heritage is, if not divinely, at least humanly authorized. The first dealers in African art were enthusiasts, pioneers; in their fatigues and pith helmets, they were hardly distinguishable from (and sometimes were) the scientists who were recording the fascinating lessons of African life and religion. They took advantage of local beliefs and tribal warfare, and they got the objects for practically nothing. At that time, of course, the African colonies belonged to *us*.

In the 1950s, when the middle class all over the Western world was awakening to the existence of art, the art of Africa served for many as an entrée. The galleries that dealt in African objects had casual, environmental interiors, or were comfortably cluttered. The dealers were often salty old chaps with hair-raising stories instead of aristocratic pretensions, and there was a good chance that the off-the-street buyer could afford *anything* the dealer had. They were happy, euphoric days of discovery and belief: the arrival of the first Bakwele masks in New York; the rediscovery of Benin; the unravelling of the symbolism of a Bambara Chi Wara mask.

With the growth of African national egos, however, the great continent discovered, with outrage, that its cultural past was being picked clean. To them, the whole burgeoning movement was just a new form of slave trade, depriving them of something that was irreplaceable – the products of their own past. At this point, the African countries began to collect their own art, to pass laws to protect it from speculation, and to limit export. But in spite of this changing attitude, a certain element of the colonial spirit still lingers – on both sides.

There is a Paris dealer, for example, who has the habit of arriving in a country with a letter which gives the impression that he is a field worker from the Musée de l'Homme. He is given diplomatic treatment, guides and equipment, which he uses to collect objects. Of these, he gives the meagrest to the national museum and departs with the country's blessing. Recently, he went to Gabon and collected twelve valuable Bakota *mbulu ngulu* sculptures. Made of hammered brass and copper and placed on baskets to guard the bones of the dead within, this type of sculpture has become extremely rare in Africa. Since the late 1950s few old examples have been seen, and the museum in Gabon has relatively few in its possession. The arrival of the sculptures in Paris caused a stir among professionals, and there seemed to be a chance that Gabon would make an official complaint. Before things could proceed far, though, it was learned that the wife of a distinguished political personage, herself an important collector, had purchased two of the sculptures. The matter was dropped.

Part of the problem is attributable to the equivocal policies of the African states themselves, their inability to evolve a coherent viewpoint. On the one hand, the governments are trying to reduce tribalism, and the strong traditions which have historically made neighbours enemies. Traditions are based on rituals, so rituals have to be wiped out. But with their extinction comes the end of the dynamic sculpture-producing tradition. Some countries have come to realize that the tribal traditions have something to do with their own national identities. And the loss of tribal art also results in the loss of much-needed money.

Many African governments seem to object to the cultural drain largely on the grounds that they have lost a good source of revenue. The traders circulate in the bush, exchanging masks and thrones for gaudy manufactured goods, transistor radios, livestock. The governments have been unable to get a cut. They look covetously on the objects, often wanting them only because they represent a possibility of profit. For the few dedicated people who have campaigned for museums and cultural programmes to protect and preserve national property, there has been titular recognition, but rarely any material back-up. To date Gambia and Guinea have no museums, Mali's only institution is a dilapidated barracks which is helping, if anything, to accelerate the destruction by termites of the objects within. Most countries have no budget for acquisition, none for field research – not even for collecting the valuable objects remaining in the hands of the local tribes, no way to tell the villagers that an old and powerful mask is worth more than a bushel of umbrellas.

The governments of the most advanced countries are often openly opposed to the lingerings of the past that tribal ethnographica implies, and have blocked even the feeble legislation intended to conserve the remnants of the old culture. Iconoclasm has sometimes followed in the wake of political upheavals, and whole styles and epochs have been the victims of bonfires in the name of progress, Westernization and extinction of outdated ways of life.

Sadly, the people who seem to benefit most are the entrepreneurs and middlemen who have little real interest in traditional African culture: the migrating African trying to beat the handicap of his money's inferiority in the West; the peripatetic Westerner making fast cash on a form of smuggling that is taken lightly back home; the old-fashioned con man. Add to this crew an enterprising Harlem black with a 'beautiful' idea about relating to his distant origins. The idea of turning South Africa into a great crafts factory is, whatever else it may be, a stupendous one. ('Why, if the Democrats want 100,000 beaded badges that spell McGovern, we could make them in two months,'[1] the African Artcraft organizer said in *Business Week*.) But is it benevolent? Or is beading McGovern badges bad not good for African art?

The ethnographic objects that we collect and isolate inside showcases as African art are different from most other forms of 'antiquities' – the objects we collect are examples of a recent and in some cases living art. A Nimba mask in a Madison Avenue gallery is dead, for the purposes of the tradition that produced it – and its death is followed by the eventual extinction of that culture itself. This happens to all cultures. But most cultures are not forced to look at their own cadavers. The exploitation of African art represents not only a pillage of the past, but also a pillage of the future.

The most important economic outgrowth of African art for Africa is the new craft industry, which is developing all over the continent. This industry takes both traditional African and transplanted European craft techniques and applies to them the vivid African imagination and sense of colour and form, to produce an enormous range of consumer products – textiles, beads, jewellery, clothing, utensils, stools and drums – all to satisfy the growing market for native crafts in the U.S. and Europe. An offshoot of this expanding craft is the assembly-line industry which produces the insipid and tasteless African sculpture which has been given the appropriate name of 'airport art.'

It can be argued that the expansion of African crafts is a positive development, in that it decreases the strain on high-quality ethnographica (and the looting problem as well) by redirecting the layman market which is just finding out about African art. But in fact, the development of African crafts seems to be a key element in the debasement of indigenous African tribal art.

Among tribal craftsmen and their heirs, the tradition of art production continues, often still passing from father to son, but the encounter with modern civilization has changed all but the surface of this tradition. While the traditional artisan's role was fixed within his tribe – generally one of social prestige, associated with the evocation of magic and power – his modern counterpart is striving to be a self-motivated artist. In his efforts, we see the struggle to dissociate the powerful expressionism of African art from the objects' context of ritual and function. A Yoruba craftsman designs doors for the U.S. Information Service in Ibadan, following the tribal style, but without the specific incarnation that a door normally implies. Given a commission to do so, he will take the fertile female image of his tribal ancestor, and turn it into a Christian Virgin and Child. But even here, where an attempt is being made to re-establish the production of real art, the object has not totally escaped the erosive influences of popular crafts. The art works of the serious artists often most resemble the souvenir-market production of their neighbours: both seem to be parodies of the real thing.

Why has African art deteriorated? Part of the responsibility lies in an inescapable historic process, the unavoidable encounter with a changing reality, and the tendency of modern civilization to assimilate everything and reflect it in its own image. But the direction which this deterioration has taken is dishearteningly influenced by the profitable art trade. One sign of this has been the dismaying development that the most traditionally cohesive tribes have begun to produce fakes; not replicas of ritual objects for modern use, but copies made to trick the eye, and sell to foreigners. Among the Dogon of Mali, for example, many examples of their ancient Tellem art have surfaced: recently made – complete with fake patinas, for the European market.

Another sign of this disintegration is the village practice of looting ancestral burial grounds for the travelling buyer. Instead of the militant protection of the chieftain's storage house, today's travellers are met with professional-looking 8″×10″ photographs of objects for sale – both new copies and original ancient works.

Tribes in certain well-frequented regions have also got the idea of putting on displays of their rituals for tourist groups: art collecting and ritual viewing have become part of the tourist's package deal. A recent article on masked dances in Tanzania describes the function of a certain dance in the yearly initiation ritual in which young men and women are admitted into adulthood, and the body of the tribe. The article describes how 'tradition emphasized the secrecy of the masked dancer. In fact it is recorded that long ago women and uninitiated boys and girls were not allowed into the inner circle during performance. This was to keep them from coming near the dancer lest they detect the human inside.'[1] Today, the article goes on to say, masked dancing has been commercialized, and is part of the regular entertainment. The yearly initiation ritual is now performed twice a week for the sake of visitors.

The travel lecturer who books total immersion package-deal visits, the Madison Avenue dealer who displays a tribal mask as if it were a Cadillac, and the British Museum's one-time lust for Benin bronzes are different aspects of a promotion which has eroded a living culture. When it is put in these terms, almost anyone would agree that such a destructive exploitation of art is a terrible excess.

And the same question occurs again and again when such atrocities occur: How did things get this way, and who is responsible?

8

ETHICS AND AFTER

The Museum's Dilemma

Although dealers and middlemen play an important role in bringing antiquities to the market, it is ultimately the collector who gives the market its impetus. The interests of the collector and of the antiquities-rich countries are thus in conflict with each other; and it is this unresolved conflict which lies behind most of the abuses described in the preceding chapters.

Of all the elements of the antiquities market, museums, the world's most important class of collectors, are probably in the most difficult and contradictory position. As public institutions they not only have a cultural responsibility to the communities which they serve, they also have a moral responsibility to the human community in general. An object acquired by a museum is not only exhibited for the immediate benefit of museum visitors, it is also preserved for the ultimate benefit of humanity as a whole.

Until recently, the collection and preservation of ancient artifacts 'for humanity' clearly meant that part of 'humanity' which inhabited the industrialized countries: the civilized centres. Traditionally, museum people have accepted this premise without questioning, or having to question it. Most antiquities came from the poorer parts of the world, and were largely unprotected by the governments on whose soil they lay. Just as Western corporations took for granted the right to exploit the raw materials of the colonial world, so it was assumed that Westerners could rightfully exploit the artifacts lying neglected in those countries. It was also felt that those artifacts would indeed be best protected in the museums of Europe and North America. Although museum curators often knew that dealers had difficulty 'getting things out' of the countries, they generally felt that the dealer's business did not concern them. (Somewhat in the way the Western consumer who eats bananas would rarely consider himself responsible for the misery on South American banana plantations.) The museum's duty was to collect the best antiquities obtainable, and the curator trusted his dealers to make such objects available to him. As far as he was concerned, the matter stopped there.

But with the recent growth in the political and economic strength of the third world, this situation has undergone a drastic revision. Source countries, often newly independent, have begun to claim not only their own natural resources, but also the artifacts found on their own soil. And for the first time, international sentiment has begun to back their claim. The fact that an object would end up 'preserved for humanity' in a Western museum is no longer reason enough to justify its export. Why not preserve it for humanity in a museum in the country of origin? The traditional rationale of exporting art objects from the colonies to the civilized centres has become invalid: the former colonies have come to consider themselves civilized centres.

Most of the antiquities on the market today have been smuggled or even stolen from the countries of origin. The best of these objects are eventually offered to Western museums; yet the museum profession has had no traditional ethical code concerning acquisition of smuggled, or even stolen art. From Napoleon onwards, the lure of fine objects has been so irresistible that museums have traditionally done anything they could get away with to acquire something of great value. As a result, much of their collecting has been done with the utmost secrecy.

The terrible increase in looting and the hostility of the source countries have only recently caused the museums of the West to review the implications of buying antiquities on the illicit market. This issue has divided the museum profession into two opposed camps: those who operate within the traditional framework of acquiring whatever objects are needed to serve their immediate community, regardless of ethical considerations; and those who, looking toward the future, see collecting as an activity which has world-wide repercussions.

'There is no right way to get a $5.5 million painting. You get it,'[1] Metropolitan Museum director Thomas Hoving says. No complications, he further elaborates, should be allowed to stand in the way of the acquisition of a really fine object. Hoving belongs to the camp of museum professionals who continue to believe that 'all great art belongs in museums' (and not in any museum, *my* museum, Hoving would further assert.) By this principle he justifies the astounding $5.5 million that the Metropolitan Museum paid in order to get the Velasquez *Portrait of Juan de Pareja* out of England to New York ('Nobody would have criticized us if the Velasquez had gone to the National Gallery.... But we wouldn't have been doing our job and we'd be wrong. Dead wrong!' he says).[2] This principle was once again used to justify the Museum's much-criticized $1 million purchase of a large Euphronius vase in spite of allegations by the Italian government that the vase had been recently discovered in an Etruscan tomb and smuggled from Italy. Although Hoving denies that the vase was smuggled, his position seems to imply that the museum would be justified in purchasing it, even if it had been. The mechanics don't matter, Hoving says: 'In ten years, all the outrageous and silly things people are saying will be forgotten. They'll say we did a beautiful thing. In ten years no one will recall that there were any issues at all.'[3]

Hoving is probably right in assuming that these incidents will soon be forgotten, and the quality of the museum's collection will remain. Although the adherents of the old system deplore the destruction of archaeological sites, they pose the argument that, once the violation is committed, the responsible museum should buy the objects to preserve them for the public.

The second camp argues that such an attitude not only aggravates the antiquities problem, but lies at its source. Since the museum is a primary consumer, they feel the museum is responsible for the actions of its suppliers; no object should be acquired or exhibited by a museum unless it has been legally exported from its country of origin.

The first museum to endorse such a standard was the University Museum of the University of Pennsylvania in Philadelphia, one of America's foremost archaeological institutions. In April 1970, this museum issued a statement that it would purchase no more art objects or antiquities unless the objects were 'accompanied by a pedigree' certifying their legal export from the source country. Recognizing the inability of the countries of origin to control antiquities smuggling, and seeing the grave results of the illicit market, the museum concluded that public institutions should exercise their own sanctions on the market.

Shortly after the University Museum declaration, an international panel of museum directors drew up an ethical acquisition code for ICOM. This code was published in 1971, and all ICOM members were encouraged to adopt it. Although European museums have given little consideration to the question, the subject has been hotly debated in the United States. In 1973, the major American professional organizations (including the Association of Art Museum Directors, and College Art Association) adopted policies censuring the purchase or acceptance as a gift, of objects which had passed through illicit channels.

Although this position of 'ethical acquisition', which is in ascendancy in America and is expected to be adopted elsewhere, is surely a step in the right direction, it too has its limitations. Because of the chaos and secrecy which presently reign on the antiquities market, no consistent pedigree for licit objects has yet been formulated, and fine distinctions are at present almost impossible to make. Further, since the application of such criteria leaves a great deal of room for interpretation, a certain amount of abuse is unavoidable. And finally, although it is known that the purchase of questionable objects feeds the illicit antiquities market, it has not been proven that restraint from such purchase necessarily has the opposite effect.

In January 1973, Dr Robert Goldwater, the distinguished late director of the Museum of Primitive Art in New York, and a leading scholar in the field, explained some of the complications that the ethical stand would pose. Doctor Goldwater voiced mixed feelings over the new policy, and gave a concrete example of the dilemma it posed for his museum. A famous Mexican private collection of pre-Columbian art was currently up for sale. The collector wished to sell the collection as a whole, or to see a core of fine objects go to an important museum, and it was probable that only a foreign museum would be able to afford such a purchase. 'There is not enough money to keep the collection in Mexico,' Goldwater said, seeming mentally to run through a list of Mexican collectors and institutions which could contribute such an effort. 'No – on the present-day market, in dollars, Mexico cannot afford it,' he said finally. 'Of course, the government will not permit the collection to be exported.'

Goldwater went on to describe the predictable result. American collectors were already commissioning dealers to get individual objects for them. Eventually the best pieces would come out underground, bought by American private collectors. The Mexican collector would make more money, perhaps, than he would have made on a single sale to an American museum, and perhaps he would then give the rest of the collection, mostly second-quality material, to a Mexican museum. 'He would prefer to see his collection together in a museum. But he has no choice in the matter. And no one has really gained. Don't forget, by the new code, we will never see *any* of these objects, even if some day the collectors who buy them want to give them to us. We know that they were illegally exported – and by ethical acquisition we are obliged to say no. We will say no, but it's going to hurt. And of course, there are other museums which will decide by then that it is just not practical to abide by this code. It's an unfortunate situation.'

Didn't Professor Goldwater feel that the American museums' cooperation would eventually lead to a better relationship with the Mexican government, and to that government's allowing more legal exports?

'It is not likely,' he said firmly, 'if past experience is any indication – and I'm not just speaking of Mexico. Do you know that more than half of what we pay for a fine African object is paid in bribes to government officials? We pay, in spite of the fact that in these countries the antiquities protection laws would often not stand up in court. We pay because everyone pays. This is the accepted way to obtain an object. Everybody within the country is making so much money that nobody is anxious to see strictly legal channels employed. It's not the serious professionals you're fighting in these countries, it's the system. The serious professionals themselves don't know how to defeat the system and the people who are getting fat on the system. Mind you, I'd love to see them try.'

Dr Goldwater spoke for an important museum which was considering the greatest objects of a class – 'unique' objects which no country is willing to part with. But even on the most modest level of the market, the museum's decision to accept ethical acquisition can be a difficult one, as Gladys Davidson Weinberg, Assistant Director of the Art and Archaeology Museum of the University of Missouri explained in a letter to the International Council of Museums:

> The discussion of the 'ethics of acquisition' by museums prompts some observations which seem relevant to the securing of real progress toward protecting 'cultural heritage'. One significant fact seems to have been ignored: that there are many kinds of museums, not simply an abstract idea which can be called a

'Museum'. Just as in economic matters there are privileged and underprivileged countries, so with regard to art and archaeology there are privileged and under-privileged museums. At one extreme are museums which are bulging storehouses of treasure, not one-tenth of which can be exhibited or, sometimes, even examined by specialists. These represent pride of possession and nothing more. At the other extreme are small museums which are compelled to acquire, piece by piece, painfully and at great expense, objects with which to teach and thus to create appreciation of art and archaeology. In between there are all sorts of museums, some rich, some poor, some relating to one country only, and some which attempt to treat 'cultural heritage' as the property of the whole world instead of that of a single nation, in the belief that frontiers are political, not cultural, divisions.

To confine the problem to an area of which I have personal knowledge, let me ask one question: what is a small university museum to do – one whose objective is to teach but whose financial means are limited. If we should sign a declaration such as that signed by the University of Pennsylvania's Museum and followed by other museums, we would in effect be signing our Museum's death warrant. Some might ask: why not acquire objects from countries which permit exports? These can be counted on the fingers of one hand. While many nations have laws providing for export of antiquities, in practice such export is next to impossible. Our museum can speak from experience, having waited seven years for the legal receipt of a small number of unimportant antiquities from a country which every year sees vast quantities of unique objects illegally exported.

In another case we have had a different experience. Noting that a European museum director . . . mentioned that he was sorry to find none of his country's antiquities represented in a single U.S. museum, we asked how we could acquire some objects from his National Museum. He replied regretfully that he knew no method of doing so.

One might suggest that a small museum . . . apply to a larger one for permanent loan or purchase. Occasionally, very occasionally, this is possible but often the lending museum's rules

> forbid the handling of material on loan, and if it cannot be handled by students, its purpose is lost.
>
> Finally, I should like to offer the opinion that a declaration forbidding the import of antiquities into the United States is pointless. Once an object has left the place where it was found, through illegal digging and without being properly recorded, its final resting place is irrelevant. The most essential matters are control by the countries which possess the antiquities, and willingness on their part to realize that we live in one world, not simply in a collection of nations whose boundaries are frequently changing. Nearly all of us in the United States have origins elsewhere; why should we not have a share in the 'cultural heritage' which belongs to all of us?[1]

Those who most strongly endorse the ethical acquisition code hope that their abstention from acquiring undocumented art will lead to this much-needed clarification within the countries themselves of what can and cannot be exported. Many such professionals have called for a complete moratorium on antiquities purchases until the situation can be stabilized. Other museums have continued to acquire judiciously, in strict compliance with the letter of the law, only to find that a modest purchase can have as strong an effect on the market as an important one.

The Art Institute of Chicago, for example, announced a major acquisition of Mayan ceramics in June 1972. The United States was, at the same time, preparing to pass a law banning the import of pre-Columbian 'mural and sculptural art' without an export permit from the source country. The ban did not, however, apply to pre-Columbian ceramics or small objects. Allen Wardwell, the curator of the Chicago museum and a strong advocate of a strict museum acquisition code, explained that 'the Institute's aim in adding to the collection has been to find objects which represent some of the artistic achievements of the Maya without having to show the more spectacular monuments such as often appear in museum collections and have been the subject of considerable controversy regarding the antiquity laws of Mexico and Guatemala. Although relatively small in scale, each of the objects shown tells something of the Mayan culture from the standpoint of its art, its religion and its customs.'[1]

The Chicago museum, in turning its collecting interest toward ceramics, was at once expressing its concern over looting on a monumental scale, and fulfilling the needs of the museum collection, which Wardwell noted was still in a relatively embryonic state. Yet, as museums began to change over to less spectacular purchases, the market accommodated itself immediately to the change. Clemency Coggins, a leader of the movement to stop museum acquisition of smuggled pre-Columbian art, commented on the effects of the smuggled sculpture ban on the U.S. market:

> In order to compensate for the loss of major sculpture, art dealers have increased their volume in ceramics and jade, and they have raised the prices of these small objects to those once asked for sculpture. Now there is big money in pots. Not long ago, there were very few fine Mayan polychrome vessels on the market. A beautifully painted potsherd once brought a good price. Now, suddenly, there are a great many fine whole vessels available. Last spring in New York, there was a stunning exhibition including 40 or 50 carved and polychrome vessels of the highest quality. All of them were, of course, without any indication of their places of origin. Each of them probably represents one largely destroyed building, although it is more likely that such a concentration of superlative objects represents countless unproductive excavations and burials discarded at the site by looters. Whole vessels and jades can be found in tombs and caches that are usually buried well inside buildings. The wanton destruction that is inevitable in the search for small objects is in many ways worse than the plundering of larger monuments.[2]

Museum professionals say that the fault lies in the voracity of a market where anything which is under heavy demand will eventually attain a high price. Dealers, however, will point out that it is museums themselves which are most ready to pay the high prices demanded, and it is the competition between museums which keeps prices up.

In reality, the two factors are interdependent. The recent prosperity and popularity of museums have provided an ideal opportunity for them to find the funds needed to improve the scope and quality of their collections. The money is there, and the desire to collect is there. Every museum acquisition stimulates another, and once a collection is formed, it takes on its own life, dictating expansion to keep apace of the latest discoveries and trends. The museum that refuses objects on moral grounds is soon left behind; the museum that buys violates its moral responsibility to the larger human community.

Even the most scrupulous institutions – archaeological museums which form the bulk of their collections from field research missions – become involved in the competition when a new kind of material comes on the market. In 1972, for example, when a totally new kind of terra cotta sculpture, coming from an amateur excavation in Mali, turned up on the market, one of the first museums to buy it was an institution that had been a pioneer in declaring its intention to buy no more objects without proof of their legal export. When asked by ICOM whether he knew about the new Malian sculpture the director of the museum sent a stunning reply: – 'Hell, yes, we know about the sculpture. We even have a large collection of it in our basement. . . . We may all know the villains in this business, but we still don't know what to do about them.'

Ethical acquisition has produced a climate where optimism is countered by resentment, and no one is certain how to proceed. Museums which would abide by the strictest rules find that they cannot; others publicly espouse adherence to the code as a way of obscuring the issue – like the director of one American museum who served on a professional committee for the drafting of a standard acquisition code while his own museum was the subject of a claim from the Indian government that two recently-acquired sculptures had been stolen from India. (The museum eventually acknowledged possession of the sculptures, after which the Indian government inexplicably dropped its claim.) Ethical acquisition has proved to be an interim relief, but not an ideal solution to the museum's dilemma. Whether a museum supports or opposes the principle, its actions are likely to bring about some unhappy consequences.

A public scandal over acquisitions can mar a museum's reputation, jeopardize its relations with source countries, and lead to the loss of large sums of money paid for purchases that must be returned. In the past few years, as acquisition scandals have become more common, the fear of criticism has become a healthy deterrent to reckless or unscrupulous buying. Public sentiment over such issues has done as much as the campaigning of serious professionals to change the museum profession's outlook toward the acquisition of antiquities.

Yet the first major scandal happened almost by accident. On 4 February, 1970, the Boston Museum of Fine Arts opened an exhibition to celebrate its centennial anniversary, an event which was to be marked by a number of important new gifts and purchases and attended by a grand publicity campaign. Among the articles that appeared in newspapers and magazines was a notice in the *New York Times* announcing the acquisition of a marvellous hoard of gold jewellery – no doubt from a princely burial chamber somewhere in the Eastern Mediterranean – which was said to be the only treasure from its period and region to be found in recent years, except for the famous Dorak treasure, which had disappeared.

Among the people who read the *Times* notice with special interest was the English reporter Peter Hopkirk, whose frequent reporting on the Middle East had made him aware of the antiquities situation. Hopkirk was by coincidence crossing the United States on his way to Mexico, where he was to report on the looting of Latin American temples and sites for *The Times* of London. When he read the announcement, he immediately wondered whether the treasure described could be from Turkey, the source of so many of the fine classical and pre-classical antiquities on the market. If the treasure was from there, or indeed from any Eastern Mediterranean country, Hopkirk reasoned, it was most likely smuggled. But Turkey, he knew, was particularly sensitive about this issue. He consulted archaeologists and scholars and learned that many of them shared his suspicion. Most of the archaeologists believed that the treasure was a recently-discovered, smuggled hoard that had indeed come from Turkey; others suspected that it was a fake, or a 'dealer's bag' of objects put together to resemble a cache. All agreed that without scientific documentation of its source, the treasure was in any case deprived of most of its scientific and educational value.

The Times asked the Boston Museum for photographs, which the museum readily furnished, expecting, no doubt, a generous coverage of their future exhibition. What appeared instead was a half-page article, under the blazing headline: 'Smuggled Treasure from Royal Tomb Turns up in Museum' – the first article to directly accuse a museum of wrong-doing in acquiring an undocumented antiquity. It is difficult to say who was more astonished at the allegation: the public or the museum itself.

The public challenged the premise that a distinguished institution could knowingly be involved in questionable dealings; the museum denounced a non-professional's right to judge what it considered a purely professional decision. Cornelius Vermeule, the museum's curator, commented condescendingly that documentation of such objects is impossible to obtain. 'One doesn't know what export controls it might have come under,' Vermeule said. 'After all, things like this are coming up at Sotheby's all the time.'[1] To which another scholar retorted that he could not remember anything like the hoard *ever* having come up at Sotheby's – 'let alone all the time.' Despite the museum's attempts to pass off the unexpected charge as a misunderstanding, the furore would not be silenced. Then, within a month, the Italian government arrested a Genoa dealer for selling and illicitly exporting another of the Boston Museum's centennial treasures, the Raphael *Portrait of Eleonora Gonzaga.* After an investigation, it was learned that a curator of the museum had himself smuggled the painting into the United States, and the portrait was eventually returned to Italy. Next the press discovered another allegedly smuggled Turkish gold hoard in the Metropolitan Museum, and revived a feud between the Turkish government and the Dumbarton Oaks Museum in Washington over that museum's acquisition of a Byzantine silver treasure from Turkey. It was evident that the press had begun, as a matter of course, to scrutinize carefully every new exhibition; even such ancient issues as the British Museum's possession of the Elgin marbles were reopened. The uproar over the Boston gold hoard, although it did not lead to any disclosures about the conditions under which the treasure had been found, or to the return of the treasure to the country of origin, had brought the principles involved in the acquisition of antiquities irreversibly before the public eye.

Such public scrutiny has led some museums to greater care, others to greater secrecy in their acquisitions. Purchases, once announced with great fanfare, are now cautiously guarded until the museum can find the right moment to unveil them. (One British Museum officer has said privately that the American museum scandals arose from their insistence on announcing their purchases so grandly. His own custom is to put a controversial object on exhibition discreetly, then draw the public's attention to it after it has been there for some time.)

For every object that causes a public scandal, there is a quantity of equally controversial objects which never reach the public's attention – some which never leave the museum basement. Some of these are kept secret because of the delicate issue of ownership; others because they are embarrassing fakes. The enormous pressure of competition between museums, which has led curators to buy under covert conditions, has also opened an outrageous market in 'museum fakes.'

One scholar has told the story of a visit she made to several museums in the United States. At the first museum she visited, she was paid the exceptional compliment of being invited to see the museum's newest 'under wraps' treasure. It was a pillar from a Buddhist site of worship in India. The scholar was surprised that she had not heard that this monument had been looted, and was immediately sceptical. She hinted subtly to the curator that the museum might want to authenticate the purchase more carefully. Later on in her visit, when invited to see another museum's recent acquisitions, she was more than a little surprised to see the same Indian pillar! At this point, she decided to verify whether the real pillar had indeed left India. She notified Indian authorities, who checked the site and discovered upon careful examination that the pillar at the original site, too, was a fake. An alert was issued, and shipments departing from India were searched – whereupon a fourth example of the same pillar was found. The original pillar has not yet been recovered, and is probably still in the workshop of the clever faker.

A London dealer, who told me of a museum which acquired a stone Siva Nataraja from India and discovered upon delivery that it was made of poured concrete, also showed me a photograph of an apparently counterfeit Buddhist statue that had been offered to him. The statue had been 'discovered' a few years before, buried in the soil in Thailand, along with two other sculptures in the same style. One was 'recovered' by the Thai government, and had been placed in a local temple, and classified as part of the monument. The other two had been 'smuggled' out of the country, and were on sale on the European market. The dealer explained to me that another common practice among Asian counterfeiters is to take a statue which has lost its head (and its potential market value), and to carve a new head, slap it on with concrete, and then pack the whole statue in mud, so that the crudeness of the modern work is not immediately apparent. The object is photographed in that condition, and the fraud is not noticed until the statue is delivered and cleaned. The difference between dealers and museums, he maintains, is that museums sometimes pay in advance.

Another common practice in south-east Asia is for temple guardians to commission fakes of a sculptured lintel or figure which is part of their temple. When dealers come through on a buying trip, the temple guardian offers to sell the piece in question saying that he will have it removed from the temple and smuggled out to the dealer. The dealer departs, and is sent the copy made for the purpose. It has been pointed out that perhaps the guardians have finally found a practical system for saving their monuments.

The acquisition of such fakes is not uncommon. But ironically, the museum policy of keeping 'hot' objects under wraps often saves them the embarrassment of having publicly to acknowledge that they have bought a fake. A Swiss museum, for example, bought an important stone head which had originally come from a famous temple in Thailand. A Thai scholar travelling in Europe was shown the head by a curator of the museum, who was anxious to have his opinion. 'This head,' the scholar drily commented, 'is listed on the Thai national inventory, but disappeared from the monument it belongs to many years ago. If it were real, I would have to report your acquisition, and we would demand that it be returned to Thailand. But since this is a very good fake – better, I think, than the one of the same head that has been in Cologne for forty years, – I will be happy to let you keep it.'

A number of museums – the Ashmolean, British Museum, Metropolitan, Louvre and Museum of Primitive Art among them – were recently caught with a series of fake ceramic vessels from the Bronze Age site of Hacilar in central Turkey. Since the site was only discovered in the late 1950s, and no vessels have been legally exported from Turkey since that time, all Haçilar objects on the market are therefore smuggled. They have nevertheless been displayed openly in museums for several years, and in 1971 a series of 66 pots was submitted to thermoluminescence testing.

Of the 66 vessels tested, 48 proved to be fakes. Then, establishing the stylistic characteristics of the fakes, scholars discovered that many more of the Haçilar objects in European museums and collections also belonged to this series. Some were even found in the Ankara Museum. Shortly after this revelation the maker of the fakes – a Turkish peasant who had once dug at Haçilar – was caught and jailed.

The acquisition of fakes by museums whose curators think they are acquiring freshly discovered objects has become a practical argument in favour of an ethical acquisition code. A museum that buys without proper documentation runs a good risk of losing money, getting caught in a legal tangle, or ending up with a shelf full of fakes. Museum competition, moreover, leads to another important abuse: the fabrication of false provenances for looted objects whose real origin the looter does not remember or wish to reveal. Karen O. Bruhns, an American archaeologist, has commented on this process in Colombia:

> 'With the beginning of an industry of making fake antiquities, some Colombian *guaqueros* ["pot-hunters"] are making a point of remembering where they got a piece and from what sort of tomb as a rough means of authenticating it if they should be questioned. . . . On the other hand, if a *guaquero* suspects that he has found a cemetery where there may be more loot, he will often deliberately give false information to protect his "claim" from poachers. Many museum artifacts in particular are known to have such false information attached to them. With the coming of archaeologists to this area, it is to be expected that more and more pieces will be falsely labelled in an effort by the *guaquero* to protect his business.'[1]

Given all these factors, the solution would seem to be: buy knowledgeably or don't buy. Yet museums must collect. And satisfactory information is usually impossible to obtain. 'I must say that in the cases where I have asked dealers for information about the origin of an object,' Gordon Washburn, the Director of Asia House in New York told me, 'the stories I've gotten have been complete fabrications.'

Because the museum must collect, relations with dealers are extremely important. Confrontations must be avoided. Some museums which have tried to cope with the problem of protecting themselves while maintaining amicable relations with dealers, have found it difficult to rationalize the two positions. The Metropolitan Museum, for example, announced that in future it would send a letter to the country of origin prior to buying any antiquity, announcing its intention to acquire the object. This system was adopted as an alternative to requiring an export certificate from the dealer. Martin Lerner, the Metropolitan curator in charge of the Far Eastern department, showed me a small relief sculpture from Kashmir which the museum had bought following the new process. I then asked him whether this practice seemed satisfactory. He told me that he found it impractical and thought the museum would soon abandon it. Most dealers who offer objects to museums will not cooperate with this screening, since it is they who stand to lose if the country demands the object back. With a private collector willing to buy every object sold to a museum, the dealer would soon decide to forego the prestige of selling to an institution, and sell privately.

Adherence to the ethical acquisition standard has also strained relations between museums and their patrons, occasionally pitting even collectors and the scholars who advise them against one another. After the adoption of the resolution in 1973, the Metropolitan Museum shelved its plans for an important exhibition of Asian art from the collection of Norton Simon. The Los Angeles County Museum was then forced to cancel another important exhibition of Asian art which was scheduled to open there and then be shown in two other American cities. The owner of the latter collection cancelled the show, he told me, because of the furore caused by Norton Simon's purchase of the Sivapuram Nataraja. Even though he said that he himself owned nothing that could be contested, he did not wish to see the public come and scrutinize his collection only for its scandal potential. At the same moment, however, one of the other museums which was to participate in the exhibition was also considering withdrawing its support, being uncertain that *any* collection of this nature could be shown without repercussions. With every such confrontation, the museum not only loses the money spent on researching and cataloguing the collection, but also risks alienating a patron it has spent years counselling, and losing forever the chance of presenting to its public a collection that the museum's experts may have been instrumental in building.

The museum is thus put in an extremely awkward position. It promotes international cultural understanding through the display of objects from other cultures, but in order to do so it must collect objects which are offered for sale without provable documentation of any kind. By refusing to purchase or even exhibit antiquities that have no legal export permit, the museums artificially limit their own collections, and deprive their public of an important artistic experience. Yet refusing to buy is the only way that a museum can arrest the increasing viciousness of the antiquities market.

The ethical acquisition stand is an idealistic gesture but cannot be expected to withstand the test of time. For it to become a practical solution to the museum's dilemma, antiquities of high quality must soon become available through legal channels. Within the museum world, the conviction grows that the next move belongs to the countries whose antiquities the world has decided to save. A system of legal export must be rapidly developed and made viable.

9

RIDING WITH THE CHAUFFEUR

Why Governments Do Not Help

In most of the so-called source countries, the exploitation of antiquities is a complex issue, tied to the country's struggle to gain stability. The political, economic, and social functions of works of art are thus sometimes more important than their artistic value, and decisions that vitally concern a country's cultural heritage are often handed down by people who have no understanding or interest in the objects as art. This confusion of purpose contributes to the inconsistent and sometimes incoherent application of antiquities laws.

The professional Antiquities Officer in such countries often finds himself in an ambiguous situation. It is he who in theory directs the country's programme of scientific research, museum maintenance and export licencing, and it is he who determines how the antiquities in his country can be protected from destruction, and also enjoyed by the people. By necessity, he generally has a highly conservative and parochial point of view. Although he may understand and appreciate the demand for his country's antiquities on the international market, his own limitations and priorities prevent him from giving first consideration to this matter. He generally prefers to ignore the pressures of the international market and to concentrate on internal problems. Thus he tends to endorse or encourage repressive export laws, and to devote a large portion of his small budget to the conservation of known monuments and the maintenance of museums. First priority is given to the antiquities already under the care of the State.

Because of the narrowness of his viewpoint, the Antiquities Officer in such countries is often criticized by Westerners who feel that his country's stagnant programme and tendency toward retaliation rather than constructive action are indicative of an unwillingness to find solutions to the real problems. In fact, the director of antiquities often would like to be more cooperative, but he is just as often forced to act as he does because of political and financial inhibitions, and his decisions to undertake more progressive programmes are frequently overridden from above. For the best intentions of the antiquities department do not always coincide with the higher motives of the State.

The story told by Fernando Garavito[1] dramatically illustrates this point. In September 1970, Garavito was appointed sub-director of National Cultural Property in Colombia. He began his work energetically, hoping to strengthen the position of the State against the commercial excavators (*guaqueros*) who controlled the Colombian antiquities market. According to law, all antiquities found in the country belong to the State and must be offered to national museums before they can be sold. Usually, though, the State rarely sees antiquities of the quality that are on sale in every jewellery shop in Bogotá, and has done nothing either to stop these sales or to control the excavating done by professional diggers in the remoter provinces.

Only three weeks after taking office, Garavito was given an opportunity to act. He learned that a sale room in Bogotà, without having sought State permission, was preparing to auction off some three thousand archaeological objects – more objects than belonged to all the museums of the Institute put together. Garavito was determined to stop the sale. He began an investigation aimed at doing so, but soon learned that he was being impeded from within the Institute. Most of the board members, Garavito learned, supported the position of the auctioneer, who was even lauded as a 'promoter of culture' (*impulsador de cultura*). When Garavito persisted, his opposition changed ground and attacked him personally, bringing up the fact that Garavito's recent appointment was an 'imposition' of the minister. Thus, a debate began in which Garavito was forced to defend his 'precarious permanence' in the Institute. The issue Garavito had raised – whether the State had the power to oppose the illegal sale of antiquities by private persons – was completely obscured.

The sale went on, and Garavito prudently decided to concentrate his energies on the legal side of the question. Soon he had prepared a proposal of 83 articles for a new set of 'Organic Cultural Statutes' which contained, he believed, the most urgent reforms needed for the legal protection of the country's antiquities. He presented the project in November 1971. In September of the following year, Garavito was still waiting for the Institute's opinion on his law.

'I consider that during that time, you could have formed an idea and made observations pertinent to the project which is, without doubt, fundamental,' he wrote in September 1972. 'The fact that you have completely ignored this project leads me to believe that, for the second time, I would have done better to keep my peace.'

While Garavito waited for the approval of his law, there occurred a series of scandals involving the Institute, which he attributed to the incompetence of one of its archaeologists. Garavito strongly criticized the Institute's policy in a memorandum which again called for an internal reorganization of the Institute, and a closer definition of its practices. Bureaucracy had turned upside down, he wrote, and had lost all national orientation. It was controlled by subordinate workers who had no idea of the purpose of their job.

The reply affirmed the Institute's faith in the archaeologist, whose excavations at Pupiales were 'a heroic indication of his activities, in excavating a tomb eighteen metres deep, and so doing in danger of his own life.' Garavito pointed out that the same work is done by any *guaquero*, who is not usually praised for his heroism. The trouble with those responsible, Garavito continued, was that from their eighteen-metre tomb, they had not noticed that the Institute of Culture had become a simple intermediary in the sale of archaeological objects coming from this very site of Pupiales. In December 1971, in fact, a functionary of the Institute had commissioned a party of *guaqueros* which had dug several tombs, then *sold* the products of their work to the Museo del Oro del Banco de la Republica (a semi-official museum owned by the national bank, whose collections are formed mostly by purchasing objects coming from 'accidental finds').

And as if that were not bad enough, Garavito complained, the official Institute of Culture excavations were conducted pretty much the same way. The work had been done without any scientific inventory being kept of what was found; then the objects had been packed up and sent at random to museums in the capital, without any documentation, and without permission of the local government. What the Institute was engaged in, Garavito said, was nothing more than State-authorized looting.

In order to rectify this situation, Garavito suggested that a museum be founded at the site of Pupiales. Such a local museum, he felt, would serve the people living in the region and also help to raise the scientific standard of the local excavations. What Garavito calls 'the myopia of the functionaries' prevented such a project from being undertaken. Everyone, it might be concluded, wanted the objects for his own museum. Or worse, as Garavito suggests, 'the laws are applied according to the caprice of the passing functionary, according to the good and bad moods of the passing functionary, or the influences that may sway the passing functionary.'

Garavito drew the conclusion that the Attorney-General of the country should investigate the functioning of an institute which in two years had allowed the public sale of 3000 objects, most of which were probably exported illicitly, in further violation of the national tax law; had allowed objects dug with the support of the Institute to be sold to another museum; and had failed not only to oppose commercial archaeology, but had employed the same techniques in its own work.

According to Garavito, each time he suggested that action be taken, efforts were made to silence him, and it was even hinted that his resignation would be in order. He finally did resign, and publicly denounced the government's policies, adding that this was the only way to avoid being silenced a fourth time. The Institute released a resolution accepting his resignation, and announced new candidates for the vacant post. A meeting of all the government agencies concerned was also to be convened to consider certain existing proposals (Garavito's was not among them) for a new law for the protection of cultural property, and to draw up a project for such a law. As of March 1974, no such law had yet been passed.

This incident might seem like a clear-cut case of government corruption, or simple indifference to the archaeological heritage of the country. It is also a case, however, of exasperatingly narrow-minded bureaucracy and an odd form of patriotism. In the eyes of Garavito's superiors, commercial exploitation of antiquities apparently enriched both the finder and the State; furthermore the Institute's own investigations, however unscientific, were conducted in order to obtain objects for national museums. If Colombia and Colombians stood to benefit, they seem to have reasoned, why complain?

It is rare enough that an antiquities officer has the bad luck to find himself at odds with his own colleagues; far more common is the dispute between museum professionals and the ubiquitous 'promoter of culture' – a local entrepreneur and collector who, until recently, has had free run of his country's archaeological reserve, and who is all too willing to see that it receives its due attention abroad.

In Ecuador the Banco Central has recently appropriated funds for the establishment of a new, modern museum. Although it has no regular programme of field research, the Museum has begun to collect the country's antiquities and to undertake research aimed at analyzing and expanding our knowledge of the many cultures whose products have been found in this country.

Almost simultaneous to the foundation of this museum came a tremendous growth of the market for pre-Columbian antiquities in Europe – the antiquities of Ecuador having a particular appeal, because of their rarity. And where there is a demand, one is almost sure to find an '*impulsador de cultura*'.

At a museum meeting in 1971, the director of ICOM was approached privately by the director of an important European museum. An interesting collection of fine pre-Columbian art was being circulated in Europe by an Ecuadorian foundation, he told ICOM. The curious thing about the exhibition was that the antiquities being shown seemed to be for sale. Some had, in fact, been offered to his museum. This seemed to him a strange approach for an exhibition intended to promote cultural understanding, and he asked what export laws Ecuador might have to cover this kind of situation.

ICOM's archives indicated that export laws in Ecuador were strict. All exports, except for temporary exchange or exhibition, were forbidden. Objects which were permitted to leave the country for exhibition should eventually return.

ICOM contacted the Director of the museum in Ecuador who responded immediately that no export permit had ever been issued for this collection. The foundation, moreover, was a spurious front invented to give prestige to an ordinary smuggling operation.

The European museum did not buy the objects, and museums in the United States, where the exhibition was to go next, were informed of the laws in Ecuador preventing antiquities sales abroad. In the meantime, the Ecuadorian government was able to trace and seize several more crates of objects headed for another 'exhibition' in Japan. The antiquities shown in Europe, however, were already lost.

One might conclude in such a case that too-strict laws seem to invite violation, since they unconditionally, perhaps unfairly, forbid a collector from selling his antiques on a market where he could realize their full value. Yet it should be remembered that the museums in many such countries are newly established, and their collections must be formed from objects bought in regular commerce. Every new buyer is thus in direct competition with the state. When the buyer is foreign, he can, furthermore, pay a price the local museum cannot hope to meet. In such a situation, it is difficult not to sympathize with the museum director who finds that it is against his country's best interest to open an export market in art; nor is it hard to imagine why he opposes the cultural promoter who, under the pretext of encouraging international understanding, would seek to do so.

Further to complicate the task of the antiquities officer, higher government officials tend to see art as a material symbol which can enhance diplomatic prestige and advance political relations.

This happens everywhere. There is good reason to believe, for example, that the French decision to lend the *Mona Lisa* to Japan was linked to France's effort to sell Japan a fleet of Concordes. It is similarly noteworthy that Egypt refused (during a period of cool relations) a Russian request that King Tutankhamen's tomb be shown in Moscow, only to change its mind a year later, when Russia renewed its military support to Cairo.

But although examples of art paving the way in diplomatic relations are common, the principle is often wrongly applied by the third world countries, with disastrous results. High ranking diplomats and statesmen, eager to gain international prestige, will often treat their national antiquities with conspicuous largess. Such grandiose gestures often conflict with the country's own systematic efforts to protect its antiquities. Thus the antiquities officer must not only protect his country's cultural resources from outside exploitation, he must also devote a considerable effort to preventing mistakes from within.

In June 1973, for example, General Yakuba Gowon, Head of State of Nigeria, made an official visit to England. As a gift to commemorate the occasion, General Gowon presented the Queen with a seventeenth-century bronze plaque from Nigeria's ancient kingdom of Benin. Since very few of these bronzes remain in Nigeria, this gift was naturally regarded by many Nigerians as a great cultural loss to their country. The particular inappropriateness of the gift was intensified by the fact that many of the finest examples of Benin art are already in the British Museum – having been carried off after the British Punitive Expedition which destroyed Benin City in 1897. The question has been raised time and again of whether those bronzes already in England shouldn't be returned to Nigeria; Gowon's gesture can only have weakened Nigeria's bargaining position in this issue. 'Why couldn't he have given her a horse?' one Englishman commented. 'The Queen loves horses. Even the Russians gave her a bloody horse.'

In another instance of diplomatic confusion, the Indian police requested that the US government intervene to recover a series of important sculptures which they claimed were stolen from India. One of the sculptures in question was part of a collection which had recently been bought from the Indian-American dealer Nasli Heeramaneck by the Los Angeles County Museum. Upon request from the Indian government, Interpol questioned the museum about the purchase. The museum responded that the Indian Ambassador to the United States had given his tacit approval to the purchase by presiding at the unveiling of the collection, as photographs of the opening clearly showed. The embarrassed Indian government dropped its claim.

More troubling than this dissension in the ranks over the use of cultural property is the shortage of funds which prevents most countries from developing strong independent programmes for the protection of antiquities. Handicapped by this lack of support, the antiquities official must depend on Western scholarship and Western funds for the completion of his country's most ambitious projects. But at the same time, experience has taught that no gift is given free, and the fear of concessions which will eventually be required in payment for an important favour often prevents antiquities officers from accepting much-needed aid when it is offered.

This situation is well illustrated by a story told me by an official in an Asian country, formerly under British control.

One of Britain's most distinguished archaeologists had been excavating in the Orient, and was preparing to leave for England. Before leaving, he handed a canvas sack, sealed with wire and addressed to himself in London, to the Director of Antiquities of that country.

'Could you drop this into the mail for me, old chap. Can't get it into my luggage,' the archaeologist said.

The Director of Antiquities readily accepted, but later, as he prepared the bag for shipping, realized that he had not asked what it contained – household goods, personal effects, etc., and that this information would have to be specified on the customs form. He tried to phone the archaeologist but the latter had already left for England. With great reluctance he opened the bag – and was astonished to find it full of priceless antiquities, wrapped in the dirty shirts that were being sent home. The archaeologist, with many years of experience behind him, knew that the local customs officials would not search the bag when they saw that it was shipped from the Department of Antiquities. When the discovery was made, the antiquities were simply taken out of the bag, and the bag sent on to England. Neither of the parties involved pursued the matter further.

The man who related this incident to me, an official in the country's archaeological service, has a doctorate from a prestigious American university. In the course of his work, he spent a considerable amount of time working and travelling with the British archaeologist. What he remembers most vividly about this is that whenever they drove together, to inspect a site or go to a meeting, the British scholar, in the best colonial tradition, always inisited that local officials – including my informant – rode up front with the chauffeur. 'The great British colonialist, of course, sat alone in the back.'

While it may be an exaggeration or an incident remembered from the past that would not be repeated today, this story of insult added to injury nevertheless dramatically illustrates the misunderstanding and incomprehension which lie at the root of the world antiquities problem. The Western governments expect the source countries to cooperate by making objects available to them through legal means. The source countries, regardless of their desire to stop archaeological destruction, cannot do so under the terms offered. Each side is speaking from a point of view which is barely comprehensible to the other, and the result is deadlock.

The source countries feel that they have no reliable defences by which to protect themselves against exploitation from the West. Within these countries the antiquities officer remains powerless to act, the higher policy of State doing little to help, and often much to hinder his work. He thus feels that he is pushed into subservience by the West, harassed by his own superiors, and held back by his personal limitations, and his inability to improve the quality of the work for which he is responsible.

Sometimes, lamentably, the antiquities administration's own priorities simply will not allow the government to intervene in a situation in which it could do so. In the south of India, for example, in the former state of Madras, one foreign excavating group is working. This team has spent eight years excavating the sites of two Kushan temples outside Madras, an excavation which has yielded three important sculptures which will go to an Indian museum.

Meanwhile, in New York, a large amount of new Kushan

material has recently turned up in the hands of dealers, and specialists began to wonder where it was coming from, fearing that the excavation site was being looted off-season. Not so, explained an American art historian who had visited the excavation.

The sculpture had been uncovered at a commercial building site in Madras City, and was being sold by the developer. Madras, she went on to explain, contains eighty temple mounds. As modern buildings rise, it is inevitable that such archaeological sites will be built upon. The Indian government could claim the sites for excavation, but has not; Kushan sculpture is the production of an ancient Buddhist civilization, and at present, the preservation of Hindu places of worship and excavation of important prehistoric antiquities are considered more pressing concerns. Furthermore, the financial interest behind the Madras building project is probably strong enough successfully to oppose any attempt by the Archaeological Survey to take over the site and excavate the sculptures.

Nevertheless, the objects are 'treasure trove' and by law belong to the State. The government, then, might have exercised its right to intervene and confiscate them. In fact, the Madras Museum had expressed concern, but had been able to do no more than send a single guard to the site. This guard was responsible for getting two pieces for the museum: two thirds of a large Buddha which had been sawed up for easier transport. The piece the guard failed to confiscate was, historically, the most important: the base of the sculpture, bearing an inscription.

Although the pieces in New York can be said to have been illegally sold and exported, the Indian government is not opposing their sale. It is also well known that the Indian export system is so inefficient that no one uses it. There are state shops in India which are authorized to sell antiquities, and even these shops cannot issue export permits for the objects they sell. 'The export permit,' they tell you with a series of winks and nods which indicate that there are easier ways of getting things out of the country, 'takes at least two years to obtain.' Since the Indian government has made, until recently, little effort to control exports, there is hardly any chance of their contesting one piece out of the thousands that have been smuggled.

One solution to the problem might be to invite foreign archaeological teams to excavate such important sites, when they are discovered. But this, too, is impossible, because of tradition. Madras is considered a sacred city, and should be excavated only by Indians, foreigners are told.

The foreign team that excavates near Madras also proposed to set up a small site museum for the objects they had excavated, so that the important sculptures and the tons of ceramics and terra cotta would not lose their scientific significance by lying unidentified in some museum basement. Archaeological Survey officials were enthusiastic about this idea, but expressed doubt whether the government would allow such a museum to be built with foreign funds. And of course, the Survey has no money to build the museum itself.

A similar reply was given to the Director of an American foundation who suggested paying for a photographic inventory of all the objects in Indian museums. 'Once the photographs are published,' he was told, 'your collectors will point to them and tell their dealers, "I want this and that".' Yet the establishment of a national photographic inventory is generally deemed to be the most urgent necessity for stopping illicit traffic. And none of the countries that suffer the most are able to afford such a project.

The one channel which has functioned to establish constructive and mutually advantageous compromises is that of inter-museum exchanges. The University of Pennsylvania museum, for example, has given medieval European sculptures to India and received Indian sculptures in return; other major Western museums are beginning to negotiate similar programmes with other countries. Going beyond this bilateral exchange, many American museum directors have proposed the establishment of a floating pool of objects, chosen from among the holdings of all the participating museums, to be permanently available to others. For the first time, museums in the West are beginning to consider alternatives to outright acquisition, and are seeking less controversial – and less costly – means of enjoying objects.

As part of this trend, a staff economist for the National Council on the Arts has proposed an interesting scheme whereby American museums would announce their willingness to lease archaeological objects from the country of origin for a twenty-year period. The museums would bid competitively on the lease terms, so that the amount paid would reflect the market value of the object. A portion of the sum paid for the lease would be passed from the government of the leasing country to the finder of the object, as his reward for turning it over to the State. The rest of the money would be used for cultural purposes. But although the countries of origin are not necessarily unreceptive to such loan and exchange projects, they have reasons for feeling that these programmes are neither practical nor to their immediate benefit.

One problem with exchanges is that non-Western museums, particularly museums in Africa and the Orient, often do not have stable enough conditions to allow fragile European paintings to be exhibited. The objects loaned must thus be sturdy enough to endure extreme temperature and humidity change. This narrows the field to sculpture or ceramics, objects which are usually felt to be less interesting than paintings, and not fully representative of the West's best production.

Another drawback is that, despite the growing popularity of indigenous arts in certain countries, the citizens of many of the source countries are not yet interested in the culture of others. This limitation is shared, to some extent, by the museum officials themselves. They are also quick to point out the pressing educational needs in their countries, which make exhibiting Western art in local museums a needless luxury, particularly when one considers the cost of shipping and insuring the objects, of preparing installations and of undertaking scholarly research in an unfamiliar field.

Thus such international rapports work only to the advantage of the largest institutions and most cosmopolitan publics, in both countries. At the popular level, where education is most urgently needed, it seems that only a total change of approach can improve the situation. And such changes of approach could only be implemented from the very tops of the governments involved. Until concepts change at this level, little can be expected to change below.

UNESCO has offered the world a nearly ideal solution on which to base future policy. Its 1970 *Convention on the means of prohibiting and preventing the illicit import, export and transfer of ownership of cultural property* is a thoughtful document which outlines measures to be taken by both source and recipient countries to put an end to the illicit market in antiquities. Source countries must prepare inventories of important monuments, sites and collections; must develop an export licensing system; must allot money to scientific excavation; must announce the loss of important objects, and must publicize their laws so that people likely to export and import such objects will know the restrictions. Recipient countries should require that dealers maintain a register of transactions; must prohibit the import of unauthorized objects; and must cooperate to see illicit imports returned to the country of origin.

As of September 1974, the UNESCO Convention had been ratified by twenty-one nations: Ecuador, Bulgaria, Nigeria, Central African Republic, Kuwait, Cameroon, Cambodia, Yugoslavia, Mexico, Niger, Libya, Argentina, Iraq, Brazil, Dominican Republic, Egypt, Panama, East Germany, Poland, Jordan and Algeria. Most Western countries maintain that they cannot ratify until export certification abroad makes it possible to establish whether an object is legal or illegal. The source countries are largely unable to ratify the Convention because they are financially incapable of putting its requirements into effect.

UNESCO, for its part, insists that the burden of application lies with the countries themselves, and refuses to promote the Convention or even to develop a UNESCO export certificate which every country would recognize. The UNESCO Convention remains, then, a neat document whose usefulness is limited to the who-knows-how-distant future.

It seems that it will be a long time before a painting by Leonardo da Vinci hangs in a Turkish museum. And until Turks can experience, in Turkey, some of the universal spiritual value of a Leonardo, their views regarding the Western need for Turkish antiquities will probably not change.

Even if Western museums and source-country governments should get together, another, much less predictable element of the art market would still remain to be considered. Unlike public institutions, the private collector is not directly restricted by professional ethics, or by abstract international agreements. The private collector need not subscribe to the ethical prescriptions of public institutions or foreign governments. Except for the laws of his own country he is bound by no code of ethics but his own.

10

A PRACTICAL ISSUE

A Collector's Viewpoint

> Art is a communication channel that can take people and open them up in a unique way. . . . Art can help us not only look at ourselves, but also it makes it possible to see others with greater sensitivity and insight. It is particularly useful when cultural barriers are involved. The more we are exposed to the art of other countries, the better we are able to understand and communicate with the people from whose culture the art comes.[1]
>
> – Norton Simon

When the *New York Times* asked Norton Simon whether the Siva Nataraja of Sivapuram he had bought was smuggled, Simon is reported to have replied, 'Hell, yes, it was smuggled. I spent between $15 and $16 million over the last year on Asian art, and most of it was smuggled.'[2]* The statement stands in startling contrast to the one above it, yet to a collector of antiquities these two viewpoints are complementary. Each reflects an aspect of the important collector's position in relation to the antiquities market – one being addressed to an aesthetic, the other to a practical situation; one idealistic, the other cynical.

* This statement was later contested. When the Associated Press asked Simon for further comment, he told them that the *New York Times* statement was a distortion, but did not clarify what he had meant.

Although such apparently ambivalent feelings are shared by most major collectors, few have gone so far as publicly to admit it. To do so takes a man with a streak of impetuosity; even perhaps, a certain reforming spirit.

Or so it seemed to me. The extravagance of Norton Simon's response to Press enquiries about the Nataraja made me wonder what his views would be on the antiquities issue, and impelled me to go to see this man, who has become something of a living legend – a legend nurtured by reports of his fabulous wealth and by a reputation for enormous personal energy and almost compulsive acquisitiveness. Behind this legend I found a private collector who follows his own ethics and his own carefully considered programme of collecting, and who, remote from the public eye, seems willing to judge both himself and his public with a disarming combination of idealism and common sense, passionate candour and razor-sharp shrewdness.

Norton Simon is the founder and former president of Norton Simon Inc., a consumer products company whose various divisions manufacture Hunt tomato products, Wesson oil, *Redbook* magazine, Canada Dry beverages, and Max Factor cosmetics, and which has owned or had large interests in such diverse companies as *McCall's Magazine*, ABC-Paramount, the *Saturday Review*, the Burlington Northern Railroad, and Wheeling Steel. Simon is a self-made millionaire, whose corporate empire began with the investment of $7000 in a bankrupt orange juice bottling plant in Fullerton, California in 1931. Within the next ten years, Simon renovated the company, bought out co-investors, added tomato products to its repertory and brought its yearly profits to $9 million. He then sold this company to Hunt Brothers Packing Co. in San Francisco, and began investing in Hunt. By 1943, he was President of Hunt Brothers, at the age of thirty-six.

The steady growth of Hunt into a consumer products empire has earned Simon a reputation as a brilliant but idiosyncratic businessman, with a special talent for investing in companies bogged down in inefficiency and for building them into successful enterprises. Along the way, he has been called a 'raider' because of his style of quietly buying stock in a company, then making a sudden dramatic bid for control. He is also known as something of an iconoclast, who will break established rules in order to defeat inefficiency or hypocrisy wherever he encounters them.

The two urges, to control and to reform, seem in fact to form a kind of counterpoint in Simon's personality, and his business career has been marked by a succession of struggles and crusades. 'I have to admit that as a businessman my motivations were in conflict,' he said recently. 'I was acquisitive – in the food business I got no greater satisfaction than looking around and seeing what I could adopt from other companies – ideas and practices– to make my business more successful in money terms. I was in conflict because I wanted more dollars *and* the creative satisfaction of doing more to serve society. But on the other hand the dollars made it possible to be more creative.'[1]

In recent years, in particular, what had begun as an aggressive approach to business has been transformed into a crusade for social principles which Simon supports. By 1970, when he retired from the presidency of Norton Simon Inc., he was devoting almost all his time to the causes which had become the ruling passions of his life: education, philanthropy, and art.[2]

In 1954, with the modest purchase of three post-impressionist paintings, Norton Simon began to collect art. Ten years later he paid $15 million for the old Duveen Gallery, and with one bold stroke became one of America's most important collectors. At a sale at Christie's the next year, Simon bought the small Rembrandt *Titus* for a staggering £798,000, causing a rare moment of uproar in the London sale room when, after the painting was knocked down to his competitor (Marlborough Fine Arts), he jumped to his feet and protested: 'Mr Chairman, I have not yet finished bidding!' His complicated bidding signals, which included placing a bid with the auctioneer, bidding personally from the floor, and standing up when he was no longer interested, had confused the auctioneer, who mistakenly thought that he was out of the bidding. The bidding was reopened, and Simon gained the victory in the second round. (Simon later told a reporter that he was so upset when he thought he had lost the painting, he could hardly speak.)

By no means an isolated event, the purchase of the Rembrandt has been followed by a series of stunning acquisitions and sales which have made Norton Simon one of the most respected collectors in the world, and also one of the most controversial. He has come to be known as a man who would pay any price for something of real quality – a reputation substantiated by the number of sale room records he has set – and also as a man whose particular personality has allowed him to make his art collecting a very successful financial venture.

The focus of his collecting is not a private collection, but rather a foundation and an unorthodox museum without walls – a museum with neither galleries nor stable permanent collections, whose offices occupy a suite in a Los Angeles office building, and whose holdings have never been assembled under one roof. 'Under one roof, we'd rank with the best museums in the country,' Simon has commented. But the very idea of having the entire collection brought together would seem contrary to the Museum's own founding principles.

Although he is an ardent believer in museum viewing of art, which he feels can be even more rewarding than private ownership, Norton Simon has sharply criticized the large museums in America – for their competitiveness, for what he terms the 'egomania' that often characterizes grandiose short-term exhibitions, and for the false followers they gather. 'I don't mean to be denigrating, but art does seem to attract pseudo-intellectuals,' he said recently in an interview. 'Many around art museums live the lives of pseudo-intellectuals.'[1] When Simon founded his own museum, he decided to seek a different approach, and a way to eliminate those aspects of the museum milieu which he ardently disliked.

More like a holding company than a traditional museum, the Norton Simon Inc. Museum of Art collects art with money coming from the Norton Simon corporation and from Simon's private fortune. Rejecting the idea of a large museum building, with its costly depreciation and upkeep, and its large staff and permanent installations, the Norton Simon museum is strictly a lending institution. Controlling a collection valued at several hundred million dollars, it lends works of art to public and university museums across the United States.

According to its founding policy, the Norton Simon Inc. Museum will lend a large part of its collection to any 'solid' institution which demonstrates that it will use the art to good advantage. The loans are made for a one- or two-year period, and the Norton Simon Museum covers the cost of carriage and insurance while in transit; the recipient must provide in-place insurance, conservation, and security, and a suitable installation for the exhibition.

In December 1972, in the first important trial of this loan programme, Simon lent one hundred of the finest paintings from the Norton Simon Inc. Museum of Art and the Norton Simon Foundation to Princeton University. Other works were simultaneously hanging in museums in Houston, San Francisco, Philadelphia, Toledo, Washington, Los Angeles and Hartford. It seemed that Simon, having mastered the corporate business trust, had chosen to found a kind of huge corporate art trust, whose goal, as he expressed it, was to provide the public with 'the benefit of the same kinds of things that art has done for me.'[1]

'You see creativity,' Simon has said. 'You see that this man spent his life painting. You wonder what that expression meant to him, and you wonder what your expression means to you. What kind of nut spends his whole life painting? What kind of nut am I? What is my life expressing?'[2]

While glowing reports were coming from all quarters praising the Princeton loan exhibition, the art world was, nevertheless, buzzing with the speculation that surrounds all Simon's activities – what was he really up to, and was he not somehow making a profit even on founding a museum? For in 1971, and again in 1973, Simon had organized two stunningly successful sales at Parke-Bernet of impressionist and modern works of art, at which many works from the Norton Simon Museum and Foundation collections were disposed of. His explanation that he was 'refining his collections' seemed only to increase doubts. How could he hope to find works superior to many of those he was selling? Had he not, instead, shrewdly foreseen a future slackening of the impressionist art market? Simon replied evenly that he intended to expand the museum's holdings in Asian art. This in its turn gave rise to much gossip in the art world.

With some of the style that had given him his reputation for 'raiding' companies, Simon had become, almost overnight, one of the world's biggest buyers of Asian art. In so doing, he raised the question of how this man, famous for his unorthodox manoeuvring, would deal with the antiquities dispute. In the tiny establishment of Asian art connoisseurs, he was evoking some of the same exasperation that he had formerly evoked in business circles, and many people could not help feeling that his sudden interest in the Orient could not have come at a worse moment.

'Norton Simon! Now there's a man who has no scruples whatsoever about the situation in Asia,' one connoisseur told me. 'He has gone around to all the dealers and bought everything they had – mostly things others had refused because of provenance or because of price. Now the dealers have the idea that they can restock and maintain the prices Simon pays for everything on the market!'

'They say that Norton Simon became interested in Indian art because his second wife, Jennifer Jones, is a Yoga enthusiast,' I was told by a dealer.

In a milieu where methods of buying and collecting are prescribed with almost ritualistic precision, there were people who felt that Norton Simon had broken some basic rules. One thing that seemed particularly to offend, or to threaten, was the openness of his assault on the market, his marked lack of discretion.

In antiquities collecting, 'discretion' plays an important role, and has traditionally been a prime attribute of the brilliant collector. Success in acquiring antiquities has resulted from scrupulous efforts to convince the Asian governments that the collector's gains are not their losses. This understanding has been achieved in several ways, the motivation of the collector ranging from real philanthropy to scarcely-veiled self-interest. At one end of the spectrum are a few collectors whose passion for art seems to be the natural complement of a belief that art can serve a country as an excellent ambassador. The Rockefellers come immediately to mind – whose lavish spending on foreign cultural projects, exchanges, and research has caused it to be said that they are among the few who can 'morally afford the luxury of collecting art.'[1] Although one might object to the 'special treatment' that they may be given in their collecting, the importance of their contribution to understanding between East and West cannot be challenged.

At the other end of the spectrum, expediency rather than good intentions lies behind a collector's humanitarian gestures. This is often seen in Asia and Latin America, where the same collector who sends out looting expeditions also endows the nation's museums – thus making it difficult for the government to complain when the collector sends the best of his objects abroad for sale. In addition to supporting national cultural development (through 'field research' expeditions), and the entire economy of the local art market, these collectors also advance money to the poor, put their agents' children through school, and keep their workers out of trouble – in short, become revered pillars of the community. As distinguished collectors who also pay well, they have first choice of all that is found in the country.

In the middle ground lies the subtle case of the old-fashioned dealer-collector like the late Nasli Heeramaneck, who was at once a connoisseur and a businessman. Born in Bombay, the son of an art dealer of Parsee lineage, Heeramaneck spent his youth studying Indian art at the Victoria and Albert Museum in London. He then went to America, following the great Indian scholar and sage Ananda Coomeraswamy, who was associated with the Boston Museum of Fine Arts. In 1929, Heeramaneck opened a gallery in New York, and throughout the depression and war years quietly promoted the arts of India – this at a time when few others in India appreciated the value of their native art. Collecting for himself, he counselled and sold to other collectors as well, and is said to have built the Asian collections of the great museums in America. He has been called a 'guide, counsellor, and friend to a generation of museum men,'[1] and in 1966 when his personal collection went on exhibition at the Boston Museum, he wrote that he identified his career with 'the vision of the great and nameless artists of India whose works have come to be entrusted to me. . . . It has been my responsibility to try to select those works which best express the intensity and fervour of their devotion to God.'[2]

For all the loftiness of such ideals, Heeramaneck's movements in India were watched with some bitterness by Indian officials, and many observers of the New York scene amused themselves by speculating on how the great works of art he sold 'came to be entrusted' to Heeramaneck. The Indian government is said to have deliberated long and hard on what Heeramaneck was exporting, and on how he was getting his objects out. A rich and important man, with connections everywhere, it was assumed that he could get out of any scrape. But, the exhibition of his collection in several American museums during 1966–67 seems to have aroused particular resentment in India that so many fine objects would remain in America. It seemed evident that Heeramaneck would have to make some kind of gesture to the cultural development of India – which some said he had promoted to recognition, others that he had milked dry. It was even hinted that the ageing collector might find it difficult, in the future, to return to his native country.

Heeramaneck, however, had in mind a gesture which would prove to be precisely what was needed. He offered a group of pre-Columbian antiquities as a gift to the National Museum in New Delhi.* The museum gratefully accepted; the Indian government was satisfied. So satisfied in fact that Dr Zakir Husain, then president of India, presided at the official opening of the collection in March 1968. The collection was seen to represent 'a tremendous broadening of experience'[1] for India, and Heeramaneck died vindicated.

His death symbolized the end of an era in dealing and collecting. His collection was called the last group of Indian objects of such high quality that could be brought together privately in the Western world – a statement implying not that the supply of such objects had been exhausted, but that no one could again expect to equal Heeramaneck's ability to extract them from their native land.

When Norton Simon entered the arena, Asian art collecting was in a state of flux. The demand for fine Asian objects in the West had increased, and intimacy with Eastern ideas was making the arts of Asia more approachable. But greater demand in the West meant tighter restraint on exporting antiquities from Asia, and a greater possibility of confrontation between the collector and the country of origin. There was an implied challenge in the air, a challenge both to the impassioned collector and to the principles of Western collecting. Norton Simon is not a man to shrink from challenges. Given his personality and the delicate international situation, it was almost a foregone conclusion that he would encounter a situation like that produced by his purchase

* It is more than slightly ironic that these antiquities, too, were probably exported from their country of origin without the consent of the governments concerned.

of the Sivapuram Nataraja. The question remained: how would he deal with it when it occurred?

When I saw Norton Simon in December 1973, to hear his side of the Siva issue, he was deeply troubled by the impression of him that newspaper stories about the Nataraja conveyed. 'Look at this,' he said, holding up a back copy of a Los Angeles newspaper whose banner headline accused him of having acquired a 'hot' sculpture. 'Hot – that means stolen, doesn't it?' he reflected pensively.

I asked him whether he had known that the Nataraja was considered stolen in India when he bought it.

'That's a long story,' he said. 'Mostly, it's a matter of interpretation. We understand this sculpture came from the collection of Beman Behran. We've never heard that it was stolen from the Indian government. In fact, we've never heard *anything* from the Indian government. We've had to ask *them* to investigate.' He seemed to have jumped to the phase of the problem that was uppermost in his mind. I realized it would be best to start at the beginning, and asked him how he came to buy the Nataraja.

'I had become interested in Indian art, and I'd been collecting a lot of lesser things that I liked. Then Ben Heller offered me three great sculptures: the Sivapuram Nataraja, another Nataraja, and a Kushan pillar.' Simon spoke gravely, almost haltingly, and his hands measured off segments on the tabletop as he spoke, as if to emphasize the logical development of the affair. 'You understand, the objects were bought for the museum, not for my own collection. I didn't buy the Nataraja outright. I took a six-month option, to see if I would take it. I wanted time to consider the purchase.'

Simon began to investigate the provenance of the Nataraja. It seemed that there were at least three contradictory stories circulating as to how the sculpture had left the temple in India, and what had happened afterwards. They all concurred on one point: when it was found, the statue had bronze disease which, unless arrested, would have consumed it entirely. The temple authorities had given it to the restorer Sthapati for treatment.

From there, one story maintained that Sthapati had simply cast a copy of the sculpture, returned the copy to the temple without the knowledge of the temple guardians, and sold the original. A second account was slightly more complicated: it held that Sthapati had told the temple priests that the statue was beyond saving, and they had *sold* it to him, on condition that he made a copy for the temple.

A third version of what had happened only added to the confusion. The temple authorities, it was said, were unable to afford either a copy or extensive restoration, and had given the Nataraja to Sthapati with instructions to make a mould, melt down the original statue, and cast a copy from the same bronze. By keeping the piece intact, Sthapati had actually saved the original for posterity.

All these stories seemed equally plausible, and after six months of enquiry, Simon was no nearer the facts of the sculpture's alleged theft than when he had started. He knew that Sthapati had been arrested, but had been told that his arrest had nothing to do with the Nataraja, but rather with a string of other offences. Simon was inclined to believe the second version: that the old statue was sold by the temple guardians in exchange for a new one (a common enough practice in India). He knew, at any rate, that the piece had been in the Behran collection for a number of years. For him, then, there might be a question of smuggling, but not of theft.

Simon also knew that Ben Heller had been visited by American customs inspectors who had been asked to question him about the import of the Nataraja into the United States. But Heller told him that the inspectors had gone away satisfied as to his legal title to the piece. There seemed to be nothing irregular about its import.

I asked about the moral implications of buying such an important sculpture, since in any event the piece had almost surely been smuggled out of India, and the Indian government had since protested against its export. Didn't Simon fear that there would be repercussions when he bought this unique work of art – said to be the finest piece of Indian art outside India?

'Incidentally, that's something the Press has exaggerated, too,' he told me. 'This Nataraja has now become the "finest in existence," while really it's probably only fifth or sixth.

'I talked to people I knew, and to other dealers,' he went on, returning to the question, 'about this smuggling business. From what I heard, it seemed that all the dealers were doing the same thing – just about everything on the market comes out of these countries in the same identical way.' He noted examples of several important antiquities that had recently been bought by large museums in the West, from dealers with whom he regularly dealt. 'There's no reason to believe that these things, or other things I've bought, were any different from the Nataraja. Of course, they were probably smuggled. Nothing that comes out of India really isn't smuggled. That doesn't mean it's stolen.

'If a thing is stolen, I want to know it. I won't buy it. But as far as anything else goes, you just can't tell what's true.'

There was nothing extraordinary about this viewpoint; it is shared by most collectors and dealers in the West. Others before Simon, however, had hesitated. 'I saw the Nataraja long before Norton Simon bought it, in the basement of a museum,' another collector told me. 'Naturally I was interested – it is a spectacular thing. The museum wasn't going to buy it, and they were looking for a collector. I would have bought it, but a few days later I heard the rumours of something stolen from an Indian temple being on the market. I asked if it was the Sivapuram Nataraja, and I was told that it was. I didn't buy it, and I think most museums wouldn't have for the same reason.

'Norton Simon must have known the risk in buying the piece. I am quite sure Sherman Lee [Director of the Cleveland Museum] warned him about it.'

For Simon an additional reason to acquire the great Siva

originated with another museum. In 1972 the Metropolitan Museum was courting him with plans to hold an elaborate exhibition of his new Asian art collection. Already collecting energetically, Simon was thus given an added impetus to acquire the best Asian art available for the show. The Sivapuram Nataraja was just the kind of dramatic object to serve as the showpiece for this important exhibition. And according to an official of The Norton Simon Foundation, the museum gave more than its tacit approval of this purchase: the Met itself had held an option on the piece before it was finally offered to Simon.

Thus, encouraged on the one hand, discouraged on the other – and each side of the argument being equally persuasive and equally speculative – Simon was thrown back on his own judgement. 'The dealer gave me a guarantee that he had legal title to it in the United States,' Simon said, 'and that it was legally imported.' Since this was all the American government required, Simon decided to buy.

The planned Metropolitan exhibition was beginning to pick up the now-famous Simon rhythm, catalogues were in press, and the seventy-five objects to be shown were ready for display. Asian art scholars awaited the event with mixed emotions: a certain apprehension about the controversy the show might unleash, and an eagerness to see a fine collection. One scholar who had helped with the catalogue told me, 'I am worried about the situation in Asia. But when I saw his collection, I only thought of one thing: I can't wait to see the exhibition.'

But as final preparations for the show were being put under way, two things happened which changed the situation entirely. The acquisition of the Nataraja became a public scandal, and the Metropolitan Museum, along with other American institutions, pledged adherence to the ethical acquisition code regarding smuggled art. The Metropolitan, having undergone two recent acquisition scandals, and a public furore over their sale of a series of modern paintings, did not want to invite further criticism. It informed Simon it would have to review carefully his ownership rights of every object in the show. Simon and the museum let it be known that the exhibition plans were being renegotiated.

Again rumours circulated in the art world, speculating on what was happening. It was said that the Metropolitan had backed out mainly because Simon insisted on having the controversial Nataraja on the catalogue cover. 'Simon is known,' I heard in New York, 'for placing all kinds of conditions on his loans. He has already made them rewrite the catalogue, because he said the original one was too scholarly. [The Met later confirmed that two catalogues had been prepared, one for scholars and one for the general public.] Simon just isn't going to cooperate unless the Nataraja is in the show, with top billing.'

The museum informed the public that the exhibition could still take place – they were only waiting for clearance. Martin Lerner, curator of Far Eastern Art at the Metropolitan told me, 'As far as I'm concerned, the show will be just as important with or without the Nataraja. The Press has had their say, and I don't think there will be any more trouble. As far as we're concerned, the exhibition will go on.'

But it was also said that certain New York dealers were using all their influence to stop the show. Having been happy to sell everything they had to Simon a year before, they were now afraid that the controversy would ruin their business for ever. 'If it goes on show, even if the Nataraja is cleared, everyone will know,' I was told. 'This exhibition will rub the whole problem in everybody's faces, and the dealers don't want that.'

If the dealers feared a public airing of the issue, Simon seemed to invite one. When I asked him whether the exhibition might not create difficult relations for him in India, he expressed his belief that it could only do good. 'I am optimistic that the thing will be settled. It will come out either negative or positive, and that will help the situation. We would like to do the exhibition, if we can get the green light. Then the thing would get even more attention.' To this end, Simon's museum had asked the Indian Embassy to find out whether their government had officially claimed the sculpture as stolen. 'We're ready to negotiate with them – hear their claims to the sculpture, and to let them hear ours.'

What would he do if the sculpture was indeed stolen? I asked.

'If I find out the sculpture was stolen, I'll give it back, and get my money back from the dealer,' he said simply. 'I have said I would give it back if it would do any good – if they would see that nothing more left these countries without export clearance and a permit; and start to control export and import in this country.'

A big demand. But Simon insists that the illicit art market is an important practical issue which must be solved, not an abstract moral issue to be inconclusively debated.

'The wealthy countries should take the lead and do something about this problem,' he said. '*This* country should make laws for import and export – it's already done that with Mexico, and that situation has changed a lot. Countries like ours have got to take the initiative, control the market. If a man is a smuggler, it ought to be brought to light. After all, I think it's high time that something cultural, based on faith, was cleaned up.' Simon also said that he was actively in favour of the Unesco Convention on illicit traffic in cultural property being ratified in the United States. This would be the basis for governmental action.

Should the collector, in the meantime, consider different criteria when buying an antiquity than he would in acquiring European art? I asked.

'A collector has to buy from a dealer. It's the same everywhere. A collector buys from a dealer, a so-called reputable dealer,' Simon repeated, adding that a collector has the right to believe that the dealer is legally authorized to sell what he is offering. The governments of the West should be expected to control this market, not the buyers on it.

Would he favour stricter export control in the source countries as well?

Yes, he said. That would make things better.

Simon, a man who has formed an entire collection of 'smuggled' antiquities, surprisingly feels that the governments of the world, collectors and museums, all stand to gain from antiquities control. 'The smuggling element is seven-eighths of the price,' he said. 'If they had some control, the governments would see more money for their art, and start to let out some better pieces – like France and England do. There are plenty of antiquities left in India. . . . If they would learn to take care of them.'

It was shortsighted and impractical, he felt, for a country to hope to regain an object by tracking it to the West, and then demanding its return. 'They can't go chasing down everything they lose,' he said. 'They can't do it, physically, and they can't afford it. Like that $23,000 piece . . .' he mentioned to his assistant, perhaps referring to another object he had bought.

'If these countries would begin to control their dealers, and if they could choose the pieces they wanted, and needed, they could get money for the rest. Art trade is a big source of revenue, you know.

'The idea of these countries – like Turkey – hoarding, refusing to export anything is temporary. It will change. In Istanbul, in the museum, there are twenty-eight jewelled Sultan's swords. Why not have five, and let the rest go?'

Would the ethical code have a direct effect on him, and his collecting?

That was, indeed something his museum was concerned about. 'First the Metropolitan tells me everything's O.K. Then they go and sign this resolution, last February, and they say they can't acquire or *exhibit* any more smuggled art. It doesn't make sense. What *are* they going to exhibit?'

Simon's Asian collection, his assistant went on to explain, was always intended for the loan programme of the Norton Simon Inc. Museum. After the difficulties with the Metropolitan exhibition, Simon now hesitated to show the collection elsewhere. Which was why he hoped to see the issue of the Nataraja settled: so that the entire collection might go on public view.

'The universities aren't doing anything to help the situation, either,' he suddenly volunteered, 'by laying out money for excavations, and getting nothing in return. They used to do better, because they stole half of what was produced!'*

I asked Norton Simon if his interest in Asia would lead him to lend objects from his European collection to Asian museums.

'First the smuggling should be stopped,' he replied immediately. First things first.

A self-made multi-millionaire who runs his museum like a tight business office, Norton Simon is not a man to understand how anyone could fail to consider first things first and deal with the problem in the practical way he has outlined. In the meantime, however, he says that he intends to continue collecting, making no secrets of what he is buying, refusing to play by the rules of a game that has been outmoded. Above all, Simon disdains the rule of secretiveness that the trade has upheld for so long.

'The Kushan pillar I bought from Ben Heller, I found the pair to it at another dealer's,' he told me. 'They are both from the same temple, you see. This dealer doesn't want me to show the second one for three more years, though. He's only had it seventeen years or something. And then he doesn't want me to publish his name in the provenance, like I normally do – all that has to be straightened out. But he guarantees it's clear, legally imported into this country. So if I can straighten out these other things, it's O.K. with me.' His hands swept the matter away in the motion which denotes 'Safe'.

Whether an object like the Sivapuram Nataraja belongs in the Norton Simon Inc. Museum or in an Indian temple or museum is not a question that will be solved in a legal, cut and dried way. Nor

* This comment had much in common with a viewpoint expressed by an American university museum curator and archaeologist: 'A declaration like the one the Pennsylvania University Museum has made will probably do nothing but reinforce the determination of the countries that have the antiquities to keep them; it will not induce them to allow more exportation.'

could I see, after my interview with him, that either Norton Simon or the Indian government was clearly in the right. But Simon's insistence that the matter be in one way or another solved impressed me. Such an attitude could set a precedent, by forcing all the parties involved to evaluate their priorities and take action to see that such an incident would not be repeated. By insisting on the need for a concrete approach, Simon had taken the problem out of the realm of the abstract and almost dared the other interested parties to deal with it.

Which could be one step toward a solution. Simon, at any rate, believes that it is. He refuses to accept the view that antiquities collecting is over in the West. 'There are still plenty of things around, if you diversify,' he explains. 'Asian art is a big thing.' His self-assurance seems to imply that he expects to follow his collecting passion for the rest of his life and expects (almost demands) that roads be opened which will allow him to do so.

Eight months passed while this book was being finished and sent to press during which, of course, things happened. Bills were introduced into both houses of the American Congress to establish laws which would enable the United States to sign the Unesco Convention on illicit traffic in cultural property – the Senate bill sponsored by William Fulbright. If they passed, the United States would be the first of the big art-importing countries to sign this convention.

Meanwhile, Simon's negotiations over the Nataraja, and with the Metropolitan Museum, were proceeding, surfacing erratically in the newspapers. The Metropolitan had received a letter from a representative of the Indian government, urging that the museum should not show the sculpture. An officer of the Norton Simon museum responded that Simon was becoming disillusioned with the Metropolitan because of their hesitations and delays – there was some doubt as to whether he would allow them to show the piece at all.

In the summer of 1974, I sent a draft of this chapter to Norton Simon, and soon received a phone call from his attorney. Simon was not pleased. There were many things, he seemed to feel, that had been insufficiently explained, or distorted, and others that remained to be said. An officer of the Norton Simon Foundation was coming to Europe shortly, and if I wished, she could meet me in Paris. We made an appointment for the following week.

Then, later that same day, the telephone rang again. This time it was Norton Simon himself.

He wanted to talk about several of the points I had raised in my text, particularly about the idea of 'discretion' in the world of art dealing.

'You are familiar with this new Fulbright legislation?' he asked. 'Well. This bill was introduced in Congress, and all the dealers acted as if they wanted it. But then the lobby forces got to work – dealers and art collectors. All of a sudden, they said there was no *need* for the treaty. They have been lobbying against it, and now they have managed to sabotage the legislation. The way it looks, it won't go through at all.

'As for your chapter, you use a lot of *drama* in it, it seems to me, to get your point across. You know, dealers and collectors can be pretty nasty in what they say about each other. Maybe that's what you want. If you've got your reasons, and your facts straight, I guess that's all right. You have a right to publish what you want, and we have a right to complain, when it comes out.' But there was a bigger drama, he told me, and a bigger issue than this one sculpture: the fact that lobbying from the dealers and general bureaucracy would prevent legislation from passing, which might have brought about real progress.

'You mention the "discretion" of dealers like Heeramaneck. Well, the dealers are still making the same kind of deals he did, and lobbying in this country to be sure that this law doesn't change anything. Pieces are still coming to this country. They're still being bought by museums. Some of these museums say they're sending letters telling the countries what they're planning to acquire. I don't know if they ever send these letters – maybe they just write them so they'll have a copy for their files! They still get all the pieces they want. Maybe this is what they call 'discretion', but what they're doing is a charade!

'I have never made a secret of any deal I've made. I always quote prices in the open – I do not have secret emissaries. No deal I make will be secreted! Maybe I'm wrong, but maybe I'm an optimist...'

In December 1974 the Indian government filed suits in Los Angeles, New York and London against Norton Simon and the other principal parties who had been in possession of the Sivapuram Nataraja since its export from India. In February 1975, Simon filed countersuits for damages and 'punitive damages'. 'I think this is a landmark case,' Simon commented at the time. 'If we were to return the statue with adjudication, then all museums would be susceptible to the kind of claim made on us.'

In May 1975, a compromise was reached out of court. The Indian government agreed to allow the Norton Simon Foundation to keep and display the idol for ten years, after which it would return to India. The Foundation would have one year to decide whether to accept the agreement or go to trial.

Since the Sivapuram Nataraja left India in 1969, the Indian government has passed an antiquities act which will eventually give the State a control over antiquities dealing and export that was not formerly possible. Already the new law, and the successful resolution of this celebrated case, have stirred other Asian governments to broaden their outlook on this issue. If, in ten years, this bronze returns to India, we can only hope that its return will symbolize a new era in the treatment of the world antiquities problem, just as its loss to India was symbolic, in this decade, of the gap of understanding and good faith that must be bridged before the antiquities crisis can be resolved.

Part 3

THE ART BOOM

11

THE £100 RULE

The Growth of Art Auctions

Collectors on a large scale have always existed; the art boom has only brought them more conspicuously before the public eye. In fact, however, a more important and far-reaching consequence of the art boom may well lie in another quite different phenomenon: the enormous increase in small- and medium-scale collecting, and in popular art appreciation.

Over the last decade the world of legitimate art sales and collecting has changed radically as it has grown. At the base of this change has been the concept of art as a valuable investment. The investment principle has invaded the art market at every level, influencing modest purchases as well as grand ones. More subtly, it has come to affect, to some extent, the impact of art on everybody today.

The most important entrepreneur of art as investment has been the auction house. In developing new methods for commercializing art, the auction has become both a powerful stimulant of the continuing inflation of art prices, and a strong agent in directing contemporary taste. Although much of this has happened through the sheer momentum of the art boom, it has also resulted from the auction houses' efforts to popularize their appeal and initiate new buyers. In this effort, Sotheby's has taken a lead role;

and within Sotheby's much of the original inspiration for re-making the art market came from the idea of a man called Stanley Clark.

The portly figure of Stanley Clark is familiar to anyone who frequents the London auction room. He is the press officer of Sotheby's, the largest of the London art auction houses, and he is behind the podium at every important sale, recording figures, synthesizing and charting the effects of the sale, and calculating the best way to present this information to the press, for the advancement of Sotheby's public image. He has had an important role in constructing that image, and in making the art market what it is today. It is he who postulated the £100 rule.

Stanley Clark joined Sotheby's in 1959, at a time when no London sale room had ever mounted a public relations campaign; art auctions had never been considered newsworthy events. But things were happening to change that. First of all, the art market was changing. In New York, fervour for art buying had been growing since 1952, when the U.S. Government made donations of art to museums tax-deductible. Art collecting was becoming a profitable pastime of big businessmen and a *raison sociale* for their wives. With the George Lurcy sale at Parke-Bernet in 1957, the art auction joined museum openings and gallery showings as gala entertainment. The fashionable audience at the sale was so large that two auxiliary rooms had to be opened, linked by closed-circuit television to the central action. As the excitement of the evening rose, the crowd began to cheer the bidders on to higher and higher prices; and the knock-down of each painting was followed by enthusiastic applause. It marked the beginning of the sale room extravaganzas which would do so much to bring art before the public eye.

In London too, the climate of the art market was slowly changing. While Christie's maintained its conservative image and continued to emphasize old master sales, Sotheby's instituted sales devoted entirely to impressionist paintings, following the lead of the affluent American audience. In 1958 Sotheby's also chose a new chairman, Peter Wilson. One landmark of Wilson's first year as chairman was the celebrated Goldschmidt sale, at which seven modern paintings (two Cézannes, three Manets, a Van Gogh and a Renoir) brought an unprecedented $2,186,000 in only twenty-two minutes of bidding. This auction was the first of a series of sales which, within the next few years, would establish Sotheby's as the world's most dynamic auction house. The market lay on the brink of an explosive expansion, and it was Peter Wilson who recognized the growth potential of the chic fad for modern art.

In keeping with Wilson's business approach and his plans for Sotheby's to overtake Christie's as London's largest sale room, he made another tradition-breaking choice, the decision publicly to promote the sale of art. He saw that art, with its built-in rarity factor and new popularity as an investment, could be promoted as something whose value would endlessly rise. But in order to do so, it was necessary to establish the public's confidence in the investment value of art. Sotheby's hired a public relations officer.

Among the candidates for this position, Stanley Clark must have cut an unlikely figure. The traditional candidates were dapper, well-groomed men who had been to the right schools and moved in the proper circles – men being considered for their ability to lure the upper-class buyer to Sotheby's. Clark was jovial and unkempt, a seasoned journalist on the *Daily Telegraph* who professed to know nothing about art. He had an approach to the problem, however, which was brilliant in its simplicity, and which complemented Peter Wilson's convictions. Clark had analysed Sotheby's sales records and discovered that 60 per cent of sales were made in objects which sold for less than £100, objects 'everyman' could afford. He further noted that every man is a potential collector of sorts and that the standard of living was rising everywhere. He realized there was practically no limit to the number of modest objects that would be available for such a market. Clark's conclusion: in order to increase Sotheby's profits and establish a popular image, one needed only to bring the public into the sale room, and show them that they could afford to buy and sell. The future of the market lay not so much in setting records as it did in expansion; success depended more on the number of sales than it did on landmarks. Clark realized that once the potential buyer was awakened, the rule of supply and demand, the principle of the department store, would work for art. He managed to sell the idea to Wilson, and became the arbiter of Sotheby's programme to democratize the art market. From then on, if an object had a relation to the arts, Sotheby's was going to sell it.

Setting the ball rolling was not easy. 'Most people back then had never heard of Sotheby's of Bond Street,' Clark remembers. 'People who had, wouldn't dare come in the door. They were afraid of art. Art was for Paul Mellon and J. Paul Getty. People didn't know that they could afford it. They had to be told. We had to go out and get collectors. Well, I suppose nobody had thought of it that way, and Peter Wilson put the principle into effect. We began to give importance to the £100 lots.'

'My first time around Fleet Street, only five out of nineteen newspapers said they might be interested in covering the fine arts,' Clark told me. He shook his head, but there was the satisfaction in his look of a man whom history has proven right. 'It just wasn't easy. You know what changed things was a picture on the BBC. Sir Gerald Kelly was showing the Queen around a picture gallery. They stopped in front of a Dutch picture, a seventeenth-century interior scene, and Sir Gerald said to the Queen: "Isn't that interior a bloody marvel!" The whole nation roared! "Isn't that interior a bloody marvel!" That one remark revolutionized press coverage of art. For the first time art was talked about in the pubs.' This was the moment Clark had been waiting for.

As London newspapers began regular arts coverage, Clark began to feed them stories about the marvellous discoveries being made at Sotheby's every day. Clark felt that he was himself a model for the £100 buyer he hoped to capture (although Clark has today bought many things at Sotheby's, he still maintains that he never pays more than £100). He evolved a series of rags to riches stories that appealed to practical sense, yet were intended to melt the stoniest heart:

> A poverty-stricken old woman living on her small pension came in with a shoebox full of glass beads, begging that Sotheby's give her £2 for them. In the bottom of the box the Sotheby's expert found an ivory Saxon reliquary, missing 400 years, which a British institution was delighted to buy for £40,000. When the woman was told that she had brought in something of great value, she implored again to be given her £2 and allowed to depart in peace. Sotheby's, of course, insisted on paying her her full due, minus their modest commission. The museum could not have been happier to acquire the reliquary, which would have remained lost if the public sale room had not offered its owner a hope.[1]

As coverage increased, so did the volume of these accounts, and the flow of the trade. Newspaper stories sent people up to their lofts, and long-forgotten objects were unearthed. Sotheby's had stimulated a kind of national treasure-hunt.

> A Queensland, Australia, woman brought a goblet into Sotheby's. 'We've had this pot on the kitchen window sill in our back garden for twenty years,' she said. 'We use it to keep the door key in when we go out. Is it of any value?' It was a James I silver gilt goblet which fetched £700.[2]

The initiation of the general public to the sale room began this way. Of course, once the layman had come to the auction room to sell, he was that much more susceptible to buying. These naïve stories all have a subtle reverse appeal: if art objects can be sold so readily and successfully, they must have an inherent and stable value.

The impartiality of Sotheby's role in selling was always

emphasized, as well as the fact that a consultation cost nothing, and was without obligation.

> A London businessman bought a small shooting box in Scotland for £5000. When he visited his property he found that the former owner had left two watercolours on the wall of one room. The new owner liked them and decided to take them back to his flat in London. Some weeks later he took the watercolours to Sotheby's for examination. He was told they were by Cozens and valuable so he decided to sell. They made £5800 which meant that he had a shooting box and £800 for nothing.[1]

The auction showed itself as an unbiased and passive ground where both buyer and seller could hope to get the best possible price, and everything happened in the open.

As the prices of the most costly art began to spiral upward, this also affected modest objects. And as the number of sales increased, so the public became more convinced that art could be bought now, sold at any moment, and always at a profit. The inflation of art prices convinced many to buy immediately, before being priced out of the market. And every new sales figure reinforced the open-ended growth pattern of the art market. All these factors taken together – the investment logic, the implied prestige, the diminishing supply, the spiritual gratification of being able to afford something which had previously been considered a luxury for the rich – worked to make the common man invest.

If among the rich, art has been manipulated to make killings, the principles of art investing have been most wholly assimilated and applied by the middle class. And the auction house depends more and more on the middle class collector for its profits. In 1973, more than half of the lots sold at Sotheby's still fetched less than £100. No less impressive than the $456,000 paid in October 1973 for a Chinese 'blue and white flared bowl with medallions of dragons leaping through clouds painted on its side,' from the Ming period is the fact that profits from print and drawing sales increased 91 per cent in 1972–73, and that antique arms sales, another modest class, saw a stunning 151 per cent increase the same year, which prompted the *International Herald Tribune* sale room correspondent to write, 'Once again, this is a field which was once reserved to a handful of monomaniacs and now has been discovered by investors.'[1]

An interesting feature of the new class of art buyers is their heavy dependence on the auction room to direct their taste. The dealer or adviser who counsels the major collector and trains his eye does not exist for the average new collector of firearms, Japanese prints, and netsuke. Instead this collector learns to read the coded judgement of the auction house's expert and depends greatly on this expertise while his own connoisseurship develops. Thus he is most likely to expand his collection in the direction in which the auctions are increasing their sales promotion. The auction house, which only fifteen years ago began to assimilate the non-professional, is today the undisputed centre of the art market. As it has gained domination, it has also assumed the role of taste-maker, and now surpasses the dealer in setting the market's new trends.

There is no better example of this than the role Sotheby's has had in promoting nineteenth- and early twentieth-century decorative arts. A growing mood of nostalgia and an increased interest in the immediate past, complemented by a new scholarly interest in the art of the nineteenth century, convinced Sotheby's-Parke-Bernet (Sotheby's bought Parke-Bernet in 1964) to organize, for the first time, the sale of art from this period.

The first Art Nouveau object to be listed in Sotheby's yearly report (*Art at Auction*) was a Tiffany lamp with crab-apple shade, which sold at Parke-Bernet in October 1967 for $2800. If the price seemed incredible at the time, by 1970 the market in art nouveau had expanded so enormously that a Tiffany floorlamp with 'Laburnum shade' was worth $16,500 at Parke-Bernet. The next year, Sotheby's went further, opening a London extension called 'Sotheby's Belgravia' to sell nothing but porcelain, *objets d'art*, and English paintings dating between 1840 and 1900 –

'Victoriana'. This new sale room has become one of the most innovative and trend-setting corners of the art market.

Sotheby's Belgravia was founded for two reasons: to clear the Bond Street galleries of the clutter of nineteenth-century art that was beginning to be offered for sale, and to encourage the trend towards buying such objects – both for dealers and for the general public. 'What is intended,' reports *Art at Auction* in 1970–71, 'is a sale room dealing in all aspects of Victoriana without prejudice, where pieces which are usually relegated in obscurity to poor sales, will receive the sympathy and crucial attention they deserve. The thoroughly unworthy equation of Victoriana with junk will, through the consistently high quality of the works sold at Motcomb Street, be shown to be inarguably false.'[1] Although some of Sotheby's directors were at first sceptical of the truth of this prophecy, the unqualified success of the operation has silenced their opposition and doubts.

Marcus Linell, the dynamic young director of Sotheby's Belgravia, has played a great role in this success. Under his direction, the popularity of the new Sotheby's branch grew rapidly, surpassing everyone's expectations. Regular buyers came from both the general public and the trade. On the one hand, prices were higher, but on the other, a higher price and the stamp of Sotheby's Belgravia assured a higher resale value. The dealer would be assured of getting what he wanted – without tramping around to country sales, picking through unspecified lots, losing whole days without making a successful find. And dealers, sure of a higher price and regular turnover, began to use the sale room as a selling outlet. With more sales and more objects passing through the sale room, Sotheby's Belgravia's expertise became more reliable, constituting a real contribution to the knowledge of the objects they handled. Even the ambiance of the sale room in the lovely Belgravia quarter – a large skylighted warehouse with a neo-classical façade – works in favour of the house: the appeal of a flea market is combined with the gloss of a serious auction. Most encouraging, though, are the prices –

objects presented as serious art can almost always be found at less than £100.

One of Linell's most brilliant innovations has been the 'Collector's Item' sales, where anything from old typewriters or hurdy-gurdies to carved ships' prows may be sold in a double or triple session sale. Even dealers and collectors from overseas fly in for these sales, in spite of the fact that most of the lots are sold cheaply.

On the opening day of one of these sales, Linell directed me through an upstairs viewing room where heaps of yellowed photographs lay in disorderly piles on a large table. Linell is amused, and even a little awed by how rapidly the Collector's Item sale has achieved success. 'Old photographs, for example, used to be part of these sales,' he told me. 'Now they have become so popular that we have had to take them out. We have so many photographs to sell, that we devote special sales to them.' We went downstairs to see what would be on sale that day, passing a group of marble Victorian garden sculptures, which were waiting in the lobby for delivery to their new owner. 'Sometimes these sales even surprise us,' Linell commented, pointing to the sculptures. 'These are just the kind of thing nobody wanted a year ago. Yesterday they found a buyer, at a good price.'

The appeal of these sales is undoubtedly enhanced by the meticulously elaborate catalogues, in which 'junk' objects are presented as if they were highly desirable works of art. Lot 12 of the sale I would be attending was

> A COLLECTION OF APPROXIMATELY SEVENTY TITILLATING POSTCARDS, Christmas Cards, etc., including three mobiles of girls with elevating legs, and various others with themes on sex and lust, also a view of the interior of Maison Frida, Budapest, *the majority coloured*, c. 1900–1915
>
> [a lot]

The Belgravia catalogues are at least as elaborate as the Sotheby's

Bond Street catalogues, including such innovations as printed lists of high and low price estimates (the lot above was estimated at £15–30; at the sale it made £60), and a tear-out photograph order form through which photos may be obtained of any lot in the sale. The entries of some objects are so elaborate, in fact, that they seem almost like parodies of art historical scholarship:

> CRACKERS. A collection of thirty-three Boxes of Crackers, of various themes and seasons, including an unused Box of Gay Gordon tin and paper Crackers, Japanese Crackers and rare Emancipation Movement Crackers[1]
>
> [estimated price £20/£30; sale price £70]

In some cases, the absence of already extant scholarship has required Sotheby's Belgravia to do extensive original research, in order to give full sales documentation, the documentation becoming almost an end in itself. Such entries are often remarkable examples of the cataloguer's craft:

> NATIONAL UNION OF RAILWAYMEN. A RARE PROCESSIONAL BANNER, Painted on both sides with the words *National Union of Railwaymen, Bath Branch*, and on one side with an NUR official visiting a member's orphaned children and with four small panels of similar charitable acts, and on the other side with the entrance of the Grand Pump Room and Baths, also with four small panels, *signed on each side G. Tutill*, 83 *City Rd. London*, and bearing his brass seal; in the original storage box with the makers' *Directions for the Proper Keeping of the Banner*, within the lid, 12 ft. high, 9 ft. wide approx. *English, c. 1900.*[2]
>
> [estimated price £60/£80 – the banner was withdrawn before the sale]

Such meticulous cataloguing, of course, gives a sort of credential to the most obscure objects, which adds to the advantage of buying at Belgravia.

> A WOVEN SILK SOUVENIR HANDKERCHIEF, entitled Exposition Universelle d'Anvers en 1894, woven in orange silks and showing

the front view of the Exhibition Buildings in Antwerp, contained within an envelope labelled *Tisse pure soie par Thomas Stevens, Stevengraph Works, Coventry* (*Angleterre*)
This is apparently not recorded by Geoffrey A. Godden[1]
[tesimated price £15/£20; sale price £32]

At this sale, 219 out of 314 lots were estimated pre-sale at less than £100. Of course, as the popularity of this sale room grows, what one can get for £100 diminishes proportionately. A nineteenth-century printing press selling normally for about £150 to £200 at an English provincial auction was estimated at £300–500, and made £1500 at the sale. 'The printing press,' Linell remarked, 'is coming to be recognized as an aesthetically beautiful object in its own right.' (He also commented that such prices would generally only be paid by American buyers.)

Good business at Sotheby's Belgravia has naturally helped to promote the rage for nineteenth-century arts elsewhere. At a three-day Americana sale held at Parke-Bernet, in the Sotheby's Belgravia vein, a single Currier and Ives engraving made $6000 in November 1972. And a sale room correspondent described the sale in London at £275 of a 'hideous' Chinese gilt and lacquered bronze vase 61 inches tall as 'an interesting sidelight to the fad for Victoriana'. Of course, an increase in consumption brings a flood of objects to the sale room, everyone hoping to make their own fortune on the art boom.

This expansion is not restricted to the £100 class of objects. Julian Thompson, Director of Sotheby's Chinese Art Department, says that the owner of a lovely Chinese vase will not part with it in principle (i.e. at the £500 a dealer might offer him), but faced with a practical situation (£3000 paid for a similar vase at an auction), he will think again. Thus the rags to riches stories that established Sotheby's success early in the art boom now have a new twist, and the market has a constant supply of objects to sell.

In initiating more and more new clients, the sale rooms soon learned that every buyer gained for one class of objects was a potential collector, whose interest would expand. Another major project of the large auction houses has therefore been to bring the art market to potential new buyers, and initiate them on their own ground. Today sporting pictures are sold in Sydney, vintage cars in Los Angeles, American art in Dallas, and nineteenth-century Spanish paintings in Buenos Aires. Great American collections are sold in New York, jewellery is sold in Geneva; and when the Metropolitan Museum decided to prune its collection of ancient coins, Zurich, the capital of the world's money and ancient coin markets, was the natural choice. Meeting the prospective buyer on his own ground has proved infallibly profitable, and Christie's 1968–69 annual report summarized the psychology behind this: 'What all this amounts to is, of course, the spectacle of the world bent on the redistribution of pretty well all its more valuable possessions. Any auction house that wants to survive is bound to diversify as much as possible – opening up small-scale mirror images of the parent house in as many places as possible, breaking into new categories of saleable objects, and persuading new kinds of people that it is in their interest to sell and buy.'[1] When they explained this strategy, Christie's had, in fact, just pulled off one of the greatest coups of the recent auction market.

In 1969 Japan had its first public art auction. Christie's, determined this time to be first, had spent two and a half years organizing a sale of some 350 works of art, consisting primarily of impressionist paintings, Western arms, and Oriental works of art, to be held at a dealer's club in Tokyo; an event which entailed insuring and shipping 2½ tons of objects, preparing Japan's first auction catalogue, and publicizing the first Japanese art auction that would be open to the general public.

Japanese auctions are traditionally open only to members of the dealer profession, and the lots to be sold are not announced prior to the sale. As the sale begins, each dealer comes forward, bringing his items, one at a time, before the group. He describes the merits of what he is selling, and his speech is followed by a deluge of shouted bids. At the end, the seller can accept the highest bid, or he may reject it, politely explaining why, and what he would consider a reasonable sum, and bowing, take his object home again.

The Christie's auction was a modified European one. Although the bids were shouted in the traditional Japanese manner, there was a prepared catalogue and sales were final to the high bidders. Some 700 people attended the two-day sale, which Ivan Chance, the Chairman of Christie's, directed (in the Japanese manner) in his stockinged feet. The profits were great enough, despite the huge overhead costs, for Christie's to repeat the sale in 1970, and for Sotheby's to schedule a European-style auction in Japan in 1971. The endeavour has also more than paid off psychologically, as the 1972–73 season attested. At a single important Impressionist auction at Christie's in London 47 per cent of the lots were knocked down to Japanese buyers. The sale totalled £1,100,000. What then came to be called 'the ubiquitous Japanese' have since been visible in all the Western sale rooms – the Japanese who, because of the current monetary situation, seemed willing to pay anything for works which appealed to their taste. And, as might have been anticipated, Japanese art buyers in Europe quickly began to expand their collecting horizons from impressionist paintings to include Art Nouveau, Victoriana, nineteenth-century academic and landscape painting, and more recently, seventeenth-century landscapes and interiors. Meanwhile, Arab world oil magnates have replaced the Japanese as the sale room's neophytes, cornering the market in turn-of-the-century furniture and *objets d'art*. Although Arab buyers have, until now, been interested only in acquiring what sale room commentators judge 'typically nouveau-riche' trophies, they can be expected, in five years' time, to constitute a significant class of art buyers.

The presence of these groups in the sale room has, moreover, helped to re-inspire the Western buyer to follow their lead, and buy before it is too late. Thus, at each moment when sales begin to lag, the fuel for frantic buying is again pumped into the market.

The auction room's proven ability to revive the art market at slack moments has convinced both the general public and the professionals that anything can be promoted as art, so long as the technique of promotion is right. This capacity constantly to rejuvenate the art boom is crucial to the auction houses' success. But equally important is finding things to sell which can plausibly be described as art objects of considerable long-term worth.

Since Duveen invented the idea of collectors immortalizing themselves (and maintaining the prices they paid for art) by giving their collections to museums, the supply of objects of quality which appears on the market has decreased steadily. Every time a museum acquires an object, the number of objects available for private ownership is diminished. For the past twenty years, complaints have been heard about the disappearance of great art from the market, and predictions have been made that the end of collecting is near. The rarity of objects on the market has been further aggravated by the less spectacular investment buyer, who is likely to hold on to his purchase, as he would a stock or bond, so long as its value continues to accrue.

Since the perpetuation of a boom market depends on constant expansion – not only of prices, but also of volume of sales – the auction houses must spend a great deal of their energy on opening new sources of supply. But because great art is a limited commodity, much of what has been provided to meet the demand for art is somewhat less of an investment than the newly-trained buyer might expect.

One somewhat dubious source of supply has been of objects previously not considered art, such as the bulk of the objects which make up the Sotheby's Belgravia sales, not to mention the expanding markets for porcelain, silver, antique guns, and *objets d'art*, which no longer even arouse questions as to their intrinsic artistic value.

With such objects elevated beyond the £100 class, however, the new £100 purchase becomes a precarious investment – for the objects which can be purchased for that price are for the most part worthless as *art*. Their investment value depends upon their prices being supported by the same market which promoted them to begin with. Rising auction prices have thus led to the artistic ascendency of 'pseudo-art', without anything beyond the occasional investment index to advise the buyer that such an object may be a shaky purchase.

Another expanding class of objects has been antiquities and ethnographica, whose values are generally considered to be on the rise, as other fine objects become scarcer. Needless to say, much of the material for these sales is supplied by the black market – a fact that the auction house prefers to ignore. Regarding provenance, the auction house has no responsibility whatever, beyond satisfying itself that the seller legally owns the object to be sold. While dealers stand a chance of being publicly discredited (and are thus forced to reconsider their moral position), the auction houses have been able to go on selling objects that a dealer could not exhibit in his shop without repercussions. While the controversy was raging over the restriction of pre-Columbian imports by the America-Mexico treaty, Parke-Bernet organized the biggest pre-Columbian sale in its history, a sale which grossed $92,710. At a time when museums were condemned for buying Haçilar ware, Sotheby's was selling it openly, illustrated in its sale catalogue. Similarly, smuggled Cypriot figurines, Hellenistic jewellery, Russian icons, Javanese idols, and Benin bronzes (and fakes of all of these) come up so frequently that art price publications have become a standard looter's index to the value of the objects he finds – and the runner's index to what kind of objects he commissions to be looted.

The auction house has no interest in the moral implications of such a practice, and provides, in its unbiased system, a framework for selling anything to which the owner has convincing local title. In assuming such a role, the auction also offers a respectable locality where no one would hesitate to buy. The buyer can legitimately say that anything he bought in London comes from a 'European collection'. Generally he does not know otherwise. With objects from countries which do not permit export, the very fact that an object's origin is vague becomes a guarantee that it is a safe purchase.

Another innovation to keep art coming to the sale room has been Sotheby's price guarantee, designed to attract important selling clients to the auction room rather than the gallery. Sotheby's-Parke-Bernet have instituted the practice of guaranteeing a fixed price for really important objects which the house will pay regardless of what the painting is sold for. For this service, the seller pays 7½ per cent of his guaranteed price in addition to the normal commission. For example, if a Rembrandt is offered for sale, the house and seller may agree on a price of £100,000. If the bidding were to stop at £60,000, the seller would receive £100,000 – minus the normal commission and 7½ per cent. If the painting were to make £300,000, he would pay the extra 7½ per cent only on the £100,000 guaranteed price, and a normal commission on the rest.

With the seller receiving guarantees, the buyer, too should be given some assurance that the sale room is a safe place to make a costly purchase. Thus in September 1973, Sotheby's-Parke-Bernet announced that it would guarantee that any painting, drawing, or sculpture executed before 1870 that was sold in their sale rooms was authentically from the period under which it was catalogued. Although no promises are made regarding the actual author of the work (always a subject of contention) the buyer is assured that he has not bought a modern forgery. If he discovers that he *has* bought a forgery, he may bring it back and be reimbursed; the guarantee is valid for a period of five years after the sale.

Such assurances might give the impression that the modern sale room provides a kind of utopia where buyer and seller can both obtain the fairest deal, and operate as they choose without pressure and without doubts. But most dealers disagree. While they continue to use the auction room, dealers complain bitterly that the auction houses are usurping their clients, their methods, and their specialties, while ignoring the importance of the dealer's personal responsibility for the quality of each object he sells. The auction room, they say, is dealing, and dealing recklessly – excusing its amorality by creating an over-simplified picture of what buying and selling art is about. Such allegations are not entirely without substance. And as the world monetary situation worsens, these complaints seem to gain relevance.

The auction house, unlike the dealer, relies on continuous price expansion. It has learned to apply the principle of supply and demand, but with certain modifications; for the present art market cannot afford long periods of slack. When world markets operate by supply and demand, a major part of the marketing is usually based on constant production and obsolescence – if automobiles didn't break down and wear out, General Motors would go out of business. But in spite of the fact that the promotion and turn-over of art sales have reached enormous proportions, Sotheby's still has not found a way to manufacture art, and by definition art never becomes obsolete.

Art has also been compared to gold, as something basically rare and precious, and which has an arbitrary value. But the arbitrary price of gold is at least based on fixed weight units. The real value of art, however, is based to a large extent on belief – its material value is not based on a unit price per ounce or square inch, but on a somewhat vague notion of spiritual content. Although the art market has become increasingly systematic, nobody has yet found a way to determine, for example, the square inch value of a Rembrandt; no one is even able to judge the value of a specific Rembrandt before it sells. The reason is simple. There is no such thing as '*a* Rembrandt'. Each individual painting by Rembrandt is unique, and its price is therefore judged by a complicated formula, which takes into account such diverse factors as subject, date, size, condition, provenance, current taste, and even the merest happenstance. As Julian Agnew, the London art dealer has observed, an event like the death of a collector's grandmother can prevent him from appearing at a specific sale, and may thus change the history of the painting which he might have bought. The seller, also, is not bound by the rules of a fixed financial market. If he can't get the price he wants, he can take his work of art and go home. There is no such thing as selling at the bottom, the top or the middle of the market. Although other sales can set a general standard, every art sale, in the last analysis, is unique.

Furthermore the supply and demand principle does not apply directly to great art, in that flooding the market is not expected to reduce prices, but to raise them; whence the success of mammoth sales of high-quality works. Every object is seen as a unique work – even if the class of objects is plentiful; every work of art is uniquely valuable.

This of course begs the question: can the system fail? The answer is both yes and no, and depends on what is meant by 'failure'. The system can fail when works of art do not make the prices that are expected of them. A low price damages the credibility of the market, because when belief is lost, a work of art is virtually worthless (one is reminded of the dealer's wisdom: 'The value of a work of art is what someone will pay for it'). With prices as high as they are, the smallest failure can precipitate panic. At Christie's in November 1973, amid the oil crisis, during a moment of extreme uncertainty about the solidity of commodities with no utilitarian worth, 45 out of 133 old master paintings went unsold. Later that year the 'money pinch' further took its toll at the sale of a famous collection of Japanese *objets d'art* at Sotheby's, and at a nineteenth-century auction at Belgravia, indicating that modest buyers as well as high-level speculators were dropping out, at least temporarily. At a Christie's sale in January 1974, auction room commentators watched uncomfortably as Japanese buyers dropped out of the bidding at a fairly modest level – and speculated on what the absence of the Japanese would mean at the important spring sales. That spring, the Japanese were present, but their presence did not prevent nine significant Impressionist works from going unsold at an important auction in July. Although the failure of this sale was partly attributed to changing taste, and to the paintings being overpriced by their owners, the effect of the failure was resounding, and commentators soon began predicting a gloomy future for the art market. A downward trend can shake the art market to its core by shaking the faith of the investor on whom the market so deeply depends.

The auction house therefore has more than a passing interest in keeping up the image that art prices cannot seriously decline. Once the market declines, it can collapse. The auction house must therefore actively pursue a programme which builds faith in the future of art.

One important part of this programme is the regular publication of sales figures, announcing new record prices, increases in seasonal turnover, and even daily intake at various sales. These press releases play a large role in keeping the potential buyer in touch with the art market, and in maintaining his interest and confidence. But upon closer analysis the reader will learn that the figures often accomplish little else, and are sometimes so irrelevant as to convey a misleading image of the state of the market.

At both Sotheby's and Christie's, for example, the daily sales intake announcements are made without subtracting unsold lots from the total. And although Sotheby's subtracts unsold lots from its yearly turnover figures, Christie's makes no such adjustment. Thus the art buyer who follows sale reports may find the figures somewhat confusing. For example, although the reader learned that 45 paintings were left unsold at the Christie's old master sale in November 1973, he was also told that the total for the day was £1,273,250. This total, however, becomes far less encouraging when one considers that a full 15 per cent of the sum is accounted for by the £199,500 last bid for a Carpaccio that did not reach its reserve price. The price 'unpaid' for this painting is superior, in fact, to the price *paid* for the most expensive painting sold that day (an Avercamp ice skating scene which sold for £126,000). If the reader stops to think, he will then realize that a full third of the £1,273,250 may be accounted for by the 45 unsold paintings.

The auction house maintains that figures regarding unsold lots are kept confidential in order to protect the seller. They also might argue that their sale figures are not misleading, since the last bid for an unsold lot may be said to reflect the value of the work – someone having been willing to buy it for a price just below. But dealers and some collectors will disagree. When an important object fails to 'perform' in the sale room, they will tell you, this limits its worth, for the immediate future, on the open market. If the object is not sold by private arrangement after the sale, it becomes practically unsaleable. Thus the final bid is not only arbitrary, it may also be considerably higher than the real worth of the object after an unsuccessful sale.

Later that same December, Christie's announced a £16,531,367 turnover for the autumn season (almost £6 million more than the year before), and an increase of 127 autumn sales in 1972 to 176 in 1973. Sotheby's subsequently announced a £12 million increase over the year before (itself a record-breaking year). One might wonder how such increases could be recorded when all indications had been that sales were slack. A large part, it appears, can be credited to a proportional increase in the number of auctions hence also in objects sold. Although this volume expansion does, on the one hand, imply that the art market is healthy and sales are brisk, figures reflecting the expansion of the market tell the reader nothing about the price stability of the objects being sold – and it is in *objects* that he is investing his money, not in growth. A large volume increase is bound to boost the gross intake of the auction house, even if the prices of individual objects drop somewhat, and lots go unsold.

Nor do the percentage figures which measure the relative growth and decline of different classes of objects reveal much more than the most general buying patterns of the year. At the end of 1973–4, press releases indicated that old masters at Christie's were down 22 per cent, while 'photographica' was up 474 per cent. The reader who inferred from this that photographica might be considered a safe investment for the future, whereas old masters were falling off, would, however, have reached a fallacious conclusion. For the yearly ups and downs of old masters cannot take into account the relative importance of the works that were sold, compared to those which came into the sale room in other years. And the huge increase in an ephemeral class of objects like photographs is not an increase which can be sustained over several years, while significant art is ostensibly declining.

The wise auction-goer would do better to follow carefully the prices of individual objects in a class, forgetting about the percentage growths the auction houses periodically announce. Here, though, he may find that prices are erratic, and that the price an object attains has a lot to do with who is interested in buying and with the relative importance that the auction house attributes to the work for sale. These two criteria, in fact, might be considered the most important constituents of an art object's price at a public sale.

This is seen readily when a relatively modest object jumps to an extravagantly high price. For instance a sixteenth-century Benin bronze flute player sold for an astounding £185,000 at Sotheby's in July 1974. The previous record price for any African object had been £29,000. The 1974 price can be attributed, at least in part, to the fact that the bronze came from the well-known Ingersoll collection, was sold at the high point of the sale season, and was the showpiece of a highly important sale. Similarly, the Ming bowl that reached $456,000 in the frenzied atmosphere of Sotheby's November 1973 Chinese art sale in Hong Kong had been bought earlier the same year in London for £86,000.

But even at less significant auctions, the spotlight turned on an object can draw the attention of a collector (who will usually pay more than a dealer for something he wants), and results in a startling price increase.

An example can be made of a Russian icon which was bought by a German dealer at Sotheby's in May 1972 for £1750.[1] A year and a half later, it turned up for sale again, at Christie's. But where Sotheby's had not bothered about a photograph of the icon in the sale catalogue, Christie's illustrated it in colour, on the frontispiece. And whereas Sotheby's had called the icon the Evangelist Matthew . . . North Provincial, early seventeenth century, 'seated holding a closed book against a classical Byzantine setting,' Christie's re-identified it as the Evangelist Mark, 'seated at his desk in the act of writing the Gospel' – 'a much more poignant affair,' as *The Times* correspondent Geraldine Norman remarked. The combination of the closer attention to iconographic detail, an earlier dating (Christie's dated it to about AD 1500) and above all, the prominence in the sale (Christie's provided a full page of cataloguing) seems to have affected the price. The icon was sold for £6090 to an English collector.

One might ask whether such an object is worth what is paid for it, when promotion seems to be responsible for a large part of the price. The answer, again, must be yes and no, depending on what the buyer wants for the price he pays. To a collector, the price reflects the value he places on ownership; whereas to the buyer who hopes to place his money securely in a solid investment, the value is the price the object would be worth upon subsequent resale. Paradoxically, it is the investor who, even if he makes safer, more judicious purchases, is likely to lose.

Auction houses have also begun re-investing their profits in art-related projects which expand and reinforce their public. Thus Sotheby's has made cassette films of the 13-part series *Romantic versus Classic Art*, compiled by Lord Clark; and runs a publishing company which produces, among other things, monographs by scholars on specific kinds of art which may at the moment have particular interest in the sale room. Christie's commissions prints by contemporary artists, which are sold by mail order at modest prices (£20–£100 for prints produced in a series of 250), encouraging the buyer to think of art when he buys a gift. Sotheby's has also bought a stake in the Heritage Travel agency, which organizes posh tours to art-rich countries. The returning tourist will find the antiquities he discovered on his trip waiting for him on his return, in the London sale room.

Astute timing has also produced major Impressionist sales on the arrival of the Japanese tourist in Europe, Chinese sales to coincide with the Royal Academy exhibition of the Cultural Revolution discoveries. American Revolution memorabilia is now being stored to sell at the opening of the U.S. bicentenary festivities in 1976. The buyer, to borrow Blake's expression, would begin to fear that he is being 'connoisseured out of his senses.'

The sale room both gives impetus to and follows the trends of art viewing. Taking its lead from the public, it expands its offerings; with these expanded offerings it also enlarges its public. The auction houses have become the world's most influential dealers, and have promoted much of the art we enjoy. This is the most positive effect of the £100 rule. On the other side of the ledger, the auction houses have become frighteningly powerful dealers, on which no controls can be placed. The contemporary market, based on infinite inflation, is neither able nor willing to control its rate of growth. This is perhaps the most disquieting aspect of the £100 rule. It has at once liberated art for public consumption, and jeopardized much of that art, or priced it above the possibility of individual ownership.

12

BETTER THAN GOLD

Art and Corporate Investment

No aspect of art market finances has caused as much controversy as the recent development of art investment companies. The idea of locking art away in a vault and waiting for its value to increase has provoked repugnance from the general public, and the suspicion of professionals that art investment companies, with neither the avowed ethics of the dealer nor the public scrutiny of the auction room, are involved in all kinds of unsavoury business. Those who consider the value of art to be primarily spiritual feel that exploitation of its material worth is a form of prostitution.

From the business standpoint, however, the formation of art investment corporations was inevitable. The market on all its levels has been primarily an investor's market for well over ten years. Once the psychological barrier which opposed the exploitation of art for material return was broken, the idea of art investment entered the realm of big business. Since 1970, this idea has been applied in different ways and with varying degrees of success. Two of the most representative and successful of these operations have been Artemis and Modarco.

Artemis is a private trust which channels corporate money into the art market – a lead which many banks are beginning to follow, buying into the business of outstanding galleries and auction houses. But Artemis, instead of buying partial ownership of galleries, hires private dealers to manage their funds.

At the head of Artemis are two of Europe's most distinguished collectors and brilliant businessmen: the Baron Lambert of Brussels, and Count Artur Strachwitz of Liechtenstein. On the managing end is one of the art market's most outstanding authorities on old masters, David Carritt, who was at Christie's for many years, and who made his reputation by his exceptional ability to track down forgotten masterpieces. Carritt also has behind him a number of the world's most respected dealers, who now work for Artemis. The two bankers have established a fund of money which finances the dealers to comb the world's collections looking for exceptional purchases. What becomes of the objects depends on the market and the moment. Carritt emphasizes that Artemis has no warehouse full of paintings whose pulse is taken daily and whose disposal is carefully timed. 'In Paris, I recently bought a marvellous unrecognized Giovanni di Paolo *Baptism*, at an obscure auction. Immediately a certain columnist doomed it to "*un coffre*". In fact, I sold it to Norton Simon. If I came across an excellent Romney, I'd offer it to Paul Mellon.' Carritt explains that Artemis is a confederation of successful dealers who have a large amount of money behind them. He sees an excellent future for their business. 'American collectors are de-accessioners. They are always getting rid of their paintings. There are enough museums with good funds that a dealer who can find excellent objects can always be assured of his price.'

Many have asked why a man like Carritt, with his real love for art, would become involved in a commercial operation of this kind. (A Christie's career by contrast seems almost scholarly.) Carritt, in his sitting room, lined with art books and damask, with its sunny bay window, and baronnesses' invitations propped against the mirror, says that the equation is simple. He likes art and he likes money. 'You can like art and be a scholar. But if you also like money, there is no alternative but to be a dealer.' There is little that is revolutionary in either this view of the art market, or in Artemis's style of operation. With its constellation of outstanding experts and its large capital, one can anticipate Artemis's becoming, in a few years' time, another of the respected institutions of the art-dealing establishment.

Compared to the conservative operation of Artemis, which caters to an elite clientele, Modarco (Modern Art Collection) is a free-wheeling and daring enterprise. Backed by Swiss banks and directed almost single-handedly by Ephraim Ilin, an Israeli industrialist, the company literally invests in art, treating it as any other commodity. Modarco, Ilin explains, has a diversified and original approach to the art market.

Ephraim Ilin's interest in art started with a modern art collection which he began to assemble in 1929 (from which he has, curiously, never sold anything). His ideas about art investment may have begun with the observation that the fine objects in his collection represented so much money that one could no longer appreciate them for their artistic quality alone. Ilin, on observing this, decided to join rather than fight the trend.

A businessman, he made an estimate of an artist's life production, coming up with an average of 3000 works of art per artist. Then he took the number of museums in the world, multiplied by three or four works of art needed by a museum to represent an artist's development and range, and decided there was a critical shortage. There were not enough art works to go around. And, unlike most products the shortage could not be alleviated by any other substance; 'In art, there is no substitute,' Ilin says. If you want a painting owned by somebody else, 'you just can't have it, because there is only one.'

At this moment of crisis, Ilin discovered, the art market was also being mismanaged. Contemporary art galleries which should have been sponsoring artistic production could not devote sufficient funds to artists because of their operating costs. Dealers could not devote sufficient funds to keeping significant art circulating on the market, and competing with museums for important purchases. Art galleries, he observed, could not finance the art market on the basis of their inventories, and nobody else was financing the art market as an industry.

This was the background against which Ilin sold his industrial complex to the State, and set up Modarco, a corporation which has a double operating goal: to develop a collection which would give investors a sound investment with a 10 per cent annual dividend, and to act as a stimulant to the art market. The company's capital was placed in a prestige collection of what it calls 'masterpieces' – works of established importance, dating between 1870 and 1970. The quality of the collection was intended to attract people to invest in Modarco stock. Part of the prestige collection, which Ilin is constantly building, is sold annually to pay investor dividends (from the profits). The capital from the sale is reinvested in more 'masterpieces', in works by contemporary artists, and in backing important purchases by galleries. Thus Modarco offers a solid business investment to shareholders, and at the same time puts corporate investment funds into the art market. In theory, it draws the art market's own resources into the production of more art.

Modarco was founded in 1971. It is based in Geneva, chartered in Panama. The initial capital outlay for the company was $3 million. By the end of 1974, the capital base had grown to some $10 million. Shares in the company (whose par value was $100) were worth $182.50 at the end of 1973, at which time Ilin was again planning to enlarge the capital in order to avoid raising the price of shares. The company annually sells 15–17 per cent of its art holdings, in order to pay stockholders' dividends. With the present accrual rate of the works in the Modarco collection, Ilin hopes that he will soon be able to pay a 10 per cent dividend. The principal from the annual sales being reinvested in future purchases, the company can expand indefinitely in pace with the expanding market.

Modarco emphasizes that it has no intention of competing with dealers; it hopes, on the contrary, to support existing dealers. Unlike Artemis, Modarco does not deny that its collection is kept in storage. The Modarco collection is in a warehouse in Freeport, Geneva; the main reason for this being the obvious need for close security. Although Ilin told me that Modarco is willing to lend paintings to exhibitions (exposure enhances a painting's pedigree) no plans are being made to make the collection available to the public on a permanent basis. 'Unfortunately, today we cannot afford to maintain a museum, because the overheads would be rather expensive.' And Ilin's first responsibility is not to the public, but to his shareholders.

No catalogue exists for the Modarco collection. (Artemis's annual reports, on the other hand, read much like a major museum's – the luxuriantly illustrated objects are analysed, provenanced and tentatively attributed in a scholarly way; if the object has been sold, the purchaser's name is often listed.) Ilin feels that cataloguing is a bad idea. 'Art should not be commercialized,' he told me, in an ironic turnabout from what would seem to be company policy. This means, as he went on to explain, that too much publicity about purchases is bad for resale, since the buyer will know the date of purchase, the price paid, the conditions of sale, and other such information.

Of all the complaints levelled against art investment companies, the most common one is that the art is unappreciated as it lies in vaults, is seldom exhibited and cannot be seen even by scholars. Such a criticism could legitimately be made against Modarco. Although the company claims the title of art patron, it will do nothing to make its art accessible to the public. Ilin feels that such complaints are undeserved: 'You know, we are not the first. There is more art in Freeport, Geneva and Freeport, Basle than in all the museums of France. The owners have put it there because they are afraid of taxes, of declaring the art's value.' Modarco expresses the hope that in the future, they will be offered a place to house their collection. But to a company with a responsibility to investors the expense of putting their collection on public view is and will continue to be unjustified.

Another question which interested me was how such an enterprise directs the development of the two markets it draws upon: the market in first-rate existing art, and the contemporary market.

In the market for 'master works', Ilin told me, there is a safety of investment which does not exist on any other level of the market. 'If you have a masterpiece you can always sell it. You can never go wrong,' he said. This allows Modarco to offer a piece of the biggest action to the investor outside the art world. A modest art investor may lack the expertise to make a wise art purchase – it is well known that investment in a single object or in a minor collection can be highly risky. Art investment companies offer not only management of the investor's money, but give the modest buyer a stake in grandiose and solid purchases. In this respect, thinking always of wisely investing the shareholders' money, the art investment company may be considered an altogether new buying interest on the market for great art.

An art investment corporation like Modarco buys almost exclusively in the auction room. But unlike any of its competitors (and allied, strangely, with the auction house itself) the company strategy is to keep prices as high as possible. This it does directly through buying heavily in the sale room (although it rarely resells in the sale room – a better price can be got from a dealer!), and indirectly by bidding up certain works that it cannot buy. In December 1973 an important Picasso analytical Cubist painting, painted in 1909, was offered at Sotheby's. The painting was sold to a New York collector, who called in his bids by telephone. Modarco was the underbidder. When I saw Mr Ilin the day after the Picasso sale, I asked him what had happened.

'I very much wanted that Picasso,' he said. 'It is a terrific painting, the only one like it that will come into the sale room for years and years. But bidding against a collector, I was not going to get it. With other people's money, you can only go so high.

I had decided before the sale I would bid £300,000.' By the end of the bidding, however, Ilin had gone up to £338,000 which the American bidder topped, winning the painting at £340,000. Aside from the excitement that seizes one at an auction, Ilin had a very good reason for continuing to raise the bid, even though he realized the collector would outbid him. Modarco already owns an early Picasso gouache painted in 1909, which it bought for $75,000 in 1971. The day after the 1973 Picasso sale, Ilin estimated that his own 1909 Picasso was now worth $250,000. And a 1918 Braque Cubist painting which Modarco bought in 1971 for $150,000 Ilin now feels is worth half a million. Although he lost the Picasso, he can consider his visit to Sotheby's successful. 'I wouldn't want to sell the Braque,' he told me. 'But if somebody offers me half a million today, I sell it.'

Although not many people are affected by Modarco's manipulation of the market for Picassos, the tendency of other art investors to act similarly on the less costly market is troubling. One former French art investment company specialized in buying second-rate or contested works by masters like Renoir. Having run up the price in the auction room, and promoted these paintings through glossy publicity, the company was prepared to resell them on a market frequented by relatively inexperienced collectors who subsequently discovered that their investments were worth considerably less than they had paid for them.

Beyond the implicit possibility of investor abuse, though, the existence of numerous art investment companies with nebulous goals has given professionals another cause for concern. Such a company could easily commission the very cheap purchase of stolen paintings and smuggled antiquities. The company could keep such a work in a bank vault for a number of years without arousing suspicion, and upon expiration of the statute of limitations, sell it; all of this financed by innocent investor-shareholders. Although operations of this kind would seem imminently possible, and could account for a large number of what the police judge to be commissioned thefts, no one has yet proved that such a stolen art investment group exists.

In general, the effects of art investment companies on the market are both positive and negative. Art investment is responsible for maintaining prices at an artificially high level, thus driving the market further out of the range of the non-corporate buyer. The equilibrium of a market controlled by such interests is evidently tenuous. On the other hand, corporate art investors also tend to resell on a fairly short-term basis, keeping masterpieces in circulation. In this sense, they are better for the market than institutions, which contribute to the scarcity of saleable art.

Since the appearance of the corporate buyer, a new kind of sales counsellor has also appeared – a former dealer or auction house expert who represents a selling client, and directs the work of art towards the sale room at the moment when the highest price can be obtained. The client often pays nothing for this service – the sale room which succeeds in winning the contest for the sale of the painting gives the counsellor a commission for bringing the painting to them. Again the implications are mixed. On the one hand, the assurance of a good price will convince many more owners to part with their art – which will somewhat lessen the critical dearth of art for sale. On the other hand, what seems implied is a corporate conspiracy of middlemen who have a vested interest in always keeping prices up.

Heady as the atmosphere may seem, everyone agrees that there is a limit to which prices, already high, can be promoted.

'We can never be a half-a-billion-dollar company', Ephraim Ilin says. 'Art is not something that can be industrialized.'

David Carritt seems to share this view: 'This idea people have got of exploiting art to infinity is sheer nonsense. It simply won't work. Imagine!'

For this reason, contemporary art productions form an increasing part of Modarco's programme.

The contemporary art market, unlike the market in master

works, is not stabilized. Much of an object's value depends on vogue and local taste. An enterprising broker can buy a painting in New York and sell it 48 hours later in Basle for twice the price. A contemporary American artist's painting may be worth three times as much in the United States as in Europe; and a well-known European artist may draw little interest in America. The opposite may also hold true. The works of Mark Tobey, an American who lives in Switzerland, bring far more in Europe than in New York. Not only are fluctuations of taste wider than for Old Masters, current events also can play a more important role. A significant exhibition abroad can cause a sudden upsurge in an artist's prices. The 1974 Paris exhibition of Richard Lindner, for example, led an Italian collector to pay an unheard-of $100,000 for a Lindner in New York. Prices may also fall off dramatically when an artist's works begin to look passé. In a market that is full of speculators, the art investment company is a relatively conservative one, looking like a patron among the sharks.

Modarco emphasizes its desire both to sustain the art *market* and to sponsor *artists* in their work. This may be done in several ways. As Ilin himself told me, 'We have all kinds of gimmicks – working with the dealers, working with the artists, all kinds of gimmicks.' For example, Modarco will offer a dealer substantial backing to commission a series of works by one of the artists from the dealer's stable. The artist produces a maquette for a work, and from it the dealer and Modarco co-produce the final works, splitting the profits of the sale according to the percentage of Modarco's contribution. The art investment company is in this sense both a patron of the artist and a backer of the gallery. In another circumstance, it acts as a wholesaler. An artist will be commissioned to do a limited series of original prints, sculptures, even posters, for which he is paid a lump sum. The company then wholesales the objects, selling them to galleries, or to banks and business firms for whom the purchase is something to put on the wall and also something which they feel will gain in value.

Ilin sees nothing stimulating in this latter process, which has given rise to many firms dealing in great artists' prints. 'After all, there is nothing new about a Chagall print. It is a sure thing.' This is not sponsorship of the arts, he feels. It is wholesaling pure and simple.

Modarco's artist sponsorship is more complicated, and one begins to understand what Ilin means when he talks about 'gimmicks'. One artist who is a particular favourite of Modarco's is the young Russian sculptor Alexander Zlotnik, who now works in Paris.

Zlotnik is a Surrealist sculptor, and Modarco is a collector of Surrealism; and also a ready sponsor of sound dealer purchases. Ilin described to me how there is a subtle connection between these two roles. Modarco had recently advanced funds to a dealer to buy an important Magritte that had come on the market, for a Surrealism exhibition that the gallery was mounting. The exhibition would include all the leaders of the movement – Dali, Ernst, Magritte, Tanguy – and coincidentally, Zlotnik, an unknown but promising Surrealist sculptor. In this case, Modarco had sponsored the production of a suite of engravings by Zlotnik, and the gallery showing, to which Modarco had already contributed, would be an excellent moment to show them. The gallery would exhibit the work as a kind of return favour, and a speculative venture as well. For Modarco, Zlotnik's gallery showing built his reputation, thus increasing the value of the works by him that the company already owned; for the gallery, the fact that a company like Modarco owned works by Zlotnik was itself a selling feature for the artist. And none can doubt the boon that such funding is to the artist himself.

Modarco's yearly investment in contemporary art is 5 per cent of its total expenditure, but as other works are bought and sold, the percentage of contemporary artists' productions rises steadily. From 1972 to 1973, Modarco's contemporary holdings rose from 11.8 per cent to 35 per cent. There are several young, relatively obscure artists in the collection – purely speculative choices. Other art investment companies have chosen such schools as the American hyper-realists, and even Russian contemporary realistic painters (said to be great sellers among Italian factory owners who are hoping for Russian contracts!). In these works, bought cheaply and held on a long-term basis, the art investment company expects to make its greatest profits. There is no limit to how much the price of an artist can increase, as he rises out of obscurity.

How the art investment company, supposedly an anonymous and efficient business, chooses the young artists it sponsors seems difficult to establish. Ilin emphasizes his refusal to mix his personal taste with his company's decisions: 'With other people's money, I cannot afford to have favourites', he says. On the other hand, he is the final judge regarding all art purchases and sales. Modarco has no committee of expert counsellors: 'You cannot buy art with four eyes', Ilin explains.

With the great possibility for even experts to make mistakes in the contemporary art market, one wonders what would happen should the art investor choose wrong. I asked Ilin this, and he said, 'We are looking very selectively and very carefully. I won't start from scratch with a painter. We don't have a right to do that. Zlotnik, for example, was already somebody before I bought his work. He will be a great artist, but he was already known. Henry Moore thinks very highly of his work. Henry Moore has even promised to come to his opening.'

Beyond faith, though, it is natural that the art investment company will have a vested interest in keeping its artists' reputations up – by whatever artificial means are available – and that that interest will eventually affect the market. It becomes difficult to distinguish between the dealer and the investor at this point – both are promoting an artist in whom they see a financial future, both declare that they cannot afford to place money behind aesthetic choice alone.

Although the artist evidently stands to benefit, perhaps more than anyone else, from corporate interest in contemporary art, the question must eventually be asked whether monetary backing *which anticipates a financial return* is in fact art patronage. And if so, what consequences this kind of patronage has for the market, and for the art itself.

The answer of course depends on which side of the fence you stand. One indication that investment patronage is unhealthy would seem to be the fact that it requires a tangible product which must grow in value over the years. The artist is under pressure to produce results. Time spent without tangible results is 'money wasted'. This formula, a familiar one to assembly-line production, is not generally held to be true about art. In fact, many contemporary artists are moving away from producing 'works of art', and are searching and re-evaluating experience rather than producing objects. Part of their reaction against the art object, in fact, results from their disgust at seeing the *avant garde* institutionalized and popularized by the very social group that it was created to defy. To such artists, and to the spirit of experiment with new means, the corporate investor in art is the enemy.

It can also be argued that the admittedly conservative choice of artists by corporate investors represents a kind of reactionary patronage. The corporate investor-patron is even further removed from the *avant garde* than are the radical-chic followers of every new movement; his endorsement of an art form follows not a belief in the art, but in society's acceptance of the movement. It is justifiable to ask whether such secondary support can reach the level of the vital artists who most deserve and require patronage, and whether the artists conservatively chosen for patronage will indeed turn out to be the important artists of their time.

Although art patrons have not always been distinguished connoisseurs, in the corporate investor we find the rare instance of an art patron who is self-avowedly neutral, almost anti-aesthetic, in his view of art. And since the power of this patron is constantly increasing, many people are wondering what effect he can be expected to have.

Ephraim Ilin would argue that this is just the boost the contemporary arts need. He emphasizes the need for everyone – individuals, the community, the church – to sponsor the arts (he himself has had a hand in providing art objects for the Vatican's new contemporary art museum), and says he would like to see the foundation of more companies like his own. 'I would like more and more Modarcos to be established,' Ilin told me. 'I would like to attract more people to do the same thing. Then money will be available for art, and to appreciate art. It will raise the price of art, and it will encourage others to disclose new talents.'

Not everyone agrees. One negative effect of 'smart money' on the contemporary market has of course been to remove this (perhaps last) domain where the individual modest buyer, through use of his developed aesthetic judgement, could hope to find a masterpiece at a price he could afford. When the price of a painting by an unknown young artist has been driven from $500 to $5000 the poorer amateurs are eliminated from the market. Those who can buy do so only after carefully considering the value the object will have in the future – after assuring themselves that the artist will receive the proper patronage to keep his prices up. In this sense, the art lover also subscribes, if involuntarily, to the corporate system which has come to control the arts.

The question has also been raised of whether investing in art is indeed *financially* sound. Julian Agnew, a director of Agnews, a leading London picture-dealing firm, has pointed out that 'an investment on the Stock Exchange could be expected to produce 5 per cent return in income and 10 per cent in capital appreciation per annum; thus (ignoring compound interest) the investment would triple in value over 10 years. To match this performance, a work of art must treble in capital value over the same period, since it will produce no income; it will, in fact, absorb income as it will need to be insured.'[1] Agnew further points out that reselling a work of art costs money and takes time. Dealers and auctioneers all take a commission, at a minimum of 10 per cent.

In the case of selling through a dealer, the commissioned sale requires the time necessary to find a buyer; in selling at auction, all depends on the moment, the atmosphere, and on who is present at the sale. Through an ill-timed sale, the seller can lose the profit he had hoped to gain. Moreover, most art investors do not take into account the influence of fashion; they assume that all art will eventually become rarer and more valuable. (If this proves true, it will be a development contrary to all the previous history of the art market.)

Agnew reaches the conclusion that the investor who places his money in art for any reason other than the pleasure of owning a beautiful object is likely to invest unwisely. It is only on the highest level that fortunes have been made through art speculation. Even on this level, the price depends on the seller and investor working together continually to subsidize and inflate prices. When a Picasso is bought for £300,000 with the intention of long-term speculation, it is difficult to imagine many potential buyers who will be able to afford it, when it is again offered at three times that price. And the companies investing cannot afford to let their investments decline.

Given the present faith in art and the interests behind its continued expansion, it is possible that the market really will go on growing, enabling it to support the amount of money being poured into it. On the other hand, the private buyer may eventually come to feel that great art is too expensive for him. In this case, the corporation, the art investment company and the bank will become just another set of intermediaries between the seller and the museum.

13

THE VALUE OF A REMBRANDT

Museums and Their Trust

There are people left in the world, myself among them, who stubbornly insist that there is a maximum price that any material thing is worth – a figure perhaps engraved on a tablet somewhere in Plato's divine world of forms, but real nonetheless. It is true of French wine, waterfront land, Art Nouveau paperweights, and paintings by Rembrandt. Admittedly, the desire to believe in a maximum possible price derives partly from the self-indulgence of wanting to be able to afford good French wine, a piece of waterfront land or (in one's wildest dreams) a Rembrandt. But it also derives from a belief that such things are essential features of civilized life – not purely luxury items, as they have come to be regarded.

One of the unfortunate consequences of life within an increasingly mechanized and depersonalized society – which, we are told, allows us all to afford the better things in life – is that the availability of these so-called better things cannot increase in proportion to the number of people who are able to appreciate them; thus the prices of these 'luxury goods' cannot be restrained. They rise to heights so absurd that nobody can really afford to buy unless his purchase also represents an investment. And to invest in a pleasure is corruptive: it converts an item of personal use or enjoyment into an anonymous negotiable asset. Once a reasonable price is surpassed – £3500* for a bottle of wine is a fair example – the qualities for which the thing was conceived and has always been valued can no longer be considered. It is bought and disposed of as a commodity, or as a freakish curiosity. Unspoiled land can then only be considered for its potential as a holiday resort, and even lowly paperweights are consigned to nose- and finger-printed glass cases.

The establishment of the material value of a work of art has always been a ticklish affair, based on a concordance of tangible and intangible factors. Whereas the price of a manufactured product is determined largely by the price of the materials that constitute it, the craftsmanship required to produce it, and the cost and hazard involved in marketing it, the production cost of an expensive work of art is often negligible. The considerations which determine its value are instead such intangible ones as the reputation of the artist who created the work, its importance within his *oeuvre*, the rarity of objects like it, the dictums of contemporary taste, and the money the man who wants it is able or willing to pay. The proportionate weight of these factors is different for the art of different periods and schools, but in all cases it may be fairly said that artistic significance or beauty is only one among several factors.

There are of course certain near-constants even among these intangible factors. The greatness of certain artists is so universally recognized that there is almost never any question about the desirability of their works. Rembrandt is an example of this in painting, as is Shakespeare in literature. Both are highly valued for their profound humanity, their incomparable mastery of their media, and their deep spiritual value. If one were asked to assign a material value to the work by either of these artists, the reply might be 'priceless'. But while for a Shakespeare work,

* £3540 ($9200) was paid for a jeroboam of 1929 Mouton Rothschild at a Christie's auction in New York on 23 May 1972. The buyer was a New York wine merchant.

such as a sonnet, this would be literally true, for a Rembrandt painting it would not. While the intellectual and spiritual enrichment inherent in the Shakespeare sonnet may be bought for the modest price of a book, and by anyone, the Rembrandt painting is likely to cost hundreds of thousands of dollars, and may be owned by only one person at a time.

This distinction has more than just an abstract significance, precisely because we like to think that great works of art belong to all humanity, and that their spiritual and intellectual enrichment should be universally shared. A Shakespeare sonnet, as a product of the mind which can be infinitely replicated, can easily fulfil this role. It is available to everyone in its original form: one need only spend a modest sum and one has it to read, day or night, alone or aloud to others, in happiness or sorrow. One of the qualities of a great work of art is precisely this capacity to grow and enrich under different moods, lights, and influences. It is this expansive multi-faceted quality which makes it 'priceless'.

To do the same with a Rembrandt painting is problematical. Here the possibility of seeing the painting under different moods is perhaps even more important than with the Shakespeare sonnet, for paintings are mute and yield their wealth even more slowly than poems. All well and good, if one could afford to own a Rembrandt. One could then see it under different light, and from different angles, with friends on a sunny afternoon, by lamplight in the middle of a bout of insomnia. A painting's richness changes under these different conditions, and a painting which cannot be seen under varying experiences, is truncated. Works of art that can only be seen in a museum are, despite what publicists tell us, partly lost.

The institutionalization of the world's art is, then, only a partial means of bringing art to the people; and accessibility to important works in museums is only a complement to the intimate personal contact with objects which forms the core of artistic appreciation. Indeed, the privilege of enjoying objects freely is one of the principal impulses behind all kinds of collecting.

In literature, because the work of art is not material, there is no conflict between collecting and appreciation. A first edition of Shakespeare sonnets is a collector's item, but collecting it is a pastime which has little or nothing to do with experiencing the impact of the sonnet. In the case of the Rembrandt, since there *is* only one work of art, collecting and the possibility of intimate experience are inseparable, and both are reflected in the price. But because appreciation is not the only motive for collecting, the value placed on a painting can derive only indirectly from the value of experiencing it as a work of art.

This paradox has always existed. But on the contemporary market, the balance of factors which determine value has become distorted, and the price of a Rembrandt is forced finally so high that only an institution can afford to buy it solely as an object of aesthetic worth. In fact, even institutions cannot always afford this luxury. When a painting is very expensive aesthetics comprise only one aspect of its appeal, only one part of its value to the museum. The Rembrandt *Aristotle Contemplating the Bust of Homer* in the Metropolitan Museum is a good example of this.

In November 1961, the Metropolitan Museum, bidding against the Cleveland Museum, bought the Rembrandt *Aristotle* for $2,300,000. At the time of the sale, this price was not only a world record for a painting sold at auction, it was also the first time that a single painting had brought more than one million dollars (the previous world record having been $875,000 paid for a Fragonard sold minutes before the Rembrandt). Having anticipated a price of at least a million dollars, some of the museum's trustees opposed the acquisition of the painting on the grounds that the publicity resulting from the sale would be bad for the museum, out of keeping with its image; others had cited the fact that the museum already owned thirty-one Rembrandts. But the prevalent sentiment, as expressed by Roland Redmond, then President of the Metropolitan, to director James Rorimer, was that 'it is the really great pictures that make a collection. . . .

In the long run the price will be forgotten but the picture won't.'[1]

This prediction, of course, turned out to be the near opposite of the truth. The unheard-of price and its unprecedented publicity marked this purchase as an important turning point in both the art market and the general public's consciousness of art. It also marked a new era in museum attendance. When, some weeks after the sale, the painting appeared in the Great Hall of the museum, inside a roped-off space, surrounded by guards, every day thousands of visitors queued up to file past it, curious to see a work of art that could be worth more than two million dollars. Thanks to the Rembrandt, the museum's attendance for 1961 rose by one million over the preceding year. The price of $2.3 million was a signal heard round the world, by industries, millionaires, investment companies, banks, and the ordinary populace alike. For the former, $2.3 million for a Rembrandt meant that the moment had come to 'go into' art. For the general public, it added conviction to the growing favourable feeling towards art and museums. (An art history professor in the New York area remembers that the attendance in his introductory art appreciation course doubled shortly after the Rembrandt sale – most of the new students cheerfully admitted that their interest in art had been provoked by press accounts of the Rembrandt *Aristotle*.) The purchase was not only a triumph for the Metropolitan Museum, but a triumph, it was thought, for art.

The purchase of the Rembrandt signalled a new era for the museum as well as the public. The celebrated purchase brought new pressures and responsibilities, not the least of which was the museum's need to assure its patrons (and perhaps itself) that the Rembrandt was worth the price paid. In feeling thus obliged to attract a greater public to see the painting, the Metropolitan, like many other major museums, was pointing up a curious paradox: although museums may strive for quality in the visual experience they offer, they measure their successes in terms of quantity – how many visitors they have. The success of a $2.3 million painting would be judged partly in terms of its popularity.

But once a painting is made popular, other problems present themselves. The painting must be accessible to the enormous number of people who have come exclusively to see it, but it must also be made 'visitor-proof': safeguarded against the vandalism that its celebrity may provoke. Although one of the most lauded features of the Rembrandt *Aristotle* was its beautiful surface, its translucent glazes and rich impastos, the painting was eventually put behind a sheet of glass. Already the museum was coping with the problem of diminishing returns – the more an art object is exploited, the less is its capacity for spiritual return.

Today this problem has become acute. Inside the Musée du Jeu de Paume in Paris on a summer day, one wonders whether the purpose of the visit is not to reach the end of a queue which, inexplicably, has formed inside the museum, striving to get out. And the problem is not confined only to the West. In Leningrad the attendance at the Hermitage Museum had risen in 1973 to 3.3 million a year and it was reported that 'Soviet cultural publications get bags full of mail complaining about the sheer nuisance of museum going, the discourtesy of the throngs of inconsiderate and uncultured newcomers, the hopeless overcrowding in coatrooms, the dirt and confusion.'[1] The museum staff recognizes the problem, but can find little to do about it. 'The paintings are suffering – dust, humidity from breath, changes in the air composition, and what not,' the secretary of the Hermitage has said. 'But we cannot do anything radical. Our work is still being judged by the number of people taken in. We are given a corresponding plan every year. Tourist organizations consider it their first duty to bring to us full strength, almost every tourist train coming to Leningrad.'[2]

As we have seen elsewhere, the arrival of the masses in museums has brought about a conflict of ideals – quality for the individual against access to all – and has led to the question of how to provide enough high-quality art experience to meet the expanding demand. Unfortunately, quantity seems to be prevailing over quality. Anyone who goes to museums regularly has undoubtedly had experiences similar to the following:

In Madrid's Prado one October afternoon, a few visitors were viewing the Velasquez *Las Meniñas* when a large tourist group arrived. The tour group began to crowd into the tiny room and the other visitors moved over. The guide began his presentation. At the culmination of his speech, he turned to the mirror at the back of the room, which allows the visitor to look at the painting from the viewpoint Velasquez used to paint it. Blocking his line of vision was an elderly gentleman, one of the few non-tour visitors who had remained.

'You are in the way – could you move over?' the guide said. The visitor moved closer to the wall.

'Move into the group, please,' the guide persisted.

'I have moved aside,' the visitor said, moving up to the painting.

'You will have to move into the group or move on,' said the guide. 'My group cannot see the painting with you standing in front of it.'

'I am sorry,' the visitor said, 'but I have come during my lunch time to see this painting and I will not leave.' Already another group was waiting at the door.

The argument continued. The guide was eventually joined by a museum guard who reluctantly agreed that the effect was ruined by the visitor's standing in the way. The visitor left in a huff.

At the Uffizi Gallery in Florence, a Renaissance specialist who was studying Botticelli's *Primavera* was literally pushed aside by a guide with a tour group in tow. As he backed away, the scholar recalls overhearing a member of the group saying, 'Honey, you remember this picture, don't you? We got it on Blanche Johnson's Christmas card last year.'

At the base of the art museum's inability to provide a quality experience for everybody is the fact that the present emphasis on publicity and education is twenty years out of date. It is recognized that many visitors need direction and explanation. Yet the standard museum methods for imparting understanding have become disruptive to the process of viewing art. Few major museums suffer from lack of visitors, yet museums continue religiously to count their visitors and publicize attendance increases. And large museums all over the world have become similar in three aspects: collecting and temporary exhibition take predominance over permanent display; art education of the public is actively promoted but remains marginal in the museum programme of activities; and large crowds are assumed to justify the usefulness of the museum, its social value, and its success in its collecting. The goals and the activities of the museum seem to have become circular, and a great deal of its activities devoted not to the art which the museum houses nor to its public, but to the growth of the institution itself.

The reason, of course, is that in our visually-oriented world, dominated by television and cinema, the museum has become an entrepreneur of culture as a leisure time pursuit, and a primary competitor for the public's free time. To stay abreast of the moment, the museum must constantly compete with other institutions, and with the other visual media. While it is agreed that conditions are never satisfactory for viewing the elaborate short-term exhibitions which are mounted, museums are pressed to pour more and more funds into these exhibitions, and into museum publicity. Inter-museum competition leads to the blinding process of growth for its own sake, to the mushrooming museums which can sincerely announce, as did a trustee of the Houston, Texas, museum, that their 'paramount objectives are funds to complete the Mies Van der Rohe wing of the museum, and the raising of an acquisitions endowment which will assure the Museum a competitive position in the world art market.'[1] Competition with the media leads museums to 'brilliant theatrical displays' (as the London Chinese treasures exhibition was described on its opening day by *The Times*) which often obscure and isolate single objects beyond recognition. The public is not expected to be moved by art, but rather seduced by glitter.

The value of an art object in this syndrome is largely its capacity to yield a return. Here, in a curious way, museum and auction room policy merge. The auction exploits the art object for money, the museum exploits it for prestige and self-aggrandizement. It also follows that the museum is not without a certain vested interest in the market value of art staying high: high prices reinforce a museum's prestige and strengthen the art cult.

The major museum and the art market are broadly similar. Both employ and depend on competition, proselytism, and growth for their present success. Without the bull market in art, the auction house would still exist and unobtrusively sell art; without the celebrity of the art boom, museums would still exist, and would unobtrusively display and preserve art. But neither would be happy to return to former conditions, and both are willing to employ serious promotional schemes to maintain their places.

In the auction room and in the museum, the individual's role is diminishing. But while, at the art sale, this must be accepted as a fact of life, in the museum the viewer still has a right, at least theoretically, to demand a high-quality experience. And institutions have a responsibility, theoretically, to supply it.

Visitors' complaints about museums can generally be reduced to about four points: museums are uncomfortable; museums are crowded; crowds are often organized into disruptive groups; and the displays, to an increasing extent, are unworthy of great art. But far from doing anything to correct these faults, most museums either actively cultivate their causes, or tolerate them as the by-product of some other function. When discussing these problems with a museum worker, one often encounters the same circle of logic that pervades the museum's activities.

In a conversation with the curator of an important northeastern museum in America, for example, I suggested that groups could be limited to specific times, or days, so that on other days the individual viewer would not have to be annoyed by them.

He told me that most museums could not put such a scheme into practice for logistic reasons. And besides – closing the museum to groups part of the time would reduce its attendance figures. The museum's financial allotment from the State depended on its entry figures. Thus the museum could not afford to limit the number of groups. Furthermore, groups were less of a security risk to a museum than individuals. Members of groups rarely committed acts of vandalism. For this reason, groups were desirable.

We talked about the comfort in his museum, which contained benches in the centre of every third gallery. Lack of seating, I was told, kept people moving. Chairs interrupted the traffic pattern and slowed down the rate at which visitors completed their tour. I insisted that chairs in front of the better paintings would allow an individual to study the work more attentively, and thus serve an educational function. I was told that, since every visitor could not sit in front of a painting at the same time, the idea of chairs was discriminatory, elitist.

I insisted that if facilities like seats near paintings, proper lighting, and the channeling of fast-moving viewers through the centre of the room (where the benches normally are) were improved, each visitor would be able to look intimately at one object per visit, at least.

He told me that such notions were purely theoretical. The museum was short of money.

I pointed out that the museum had just spent well over $100,000 for a painting by a living artist. He defended the purchase on the grounds that the money for it came from another fund, and was partially donated, thus being unavailable for museum improvement. (Which is quite true, for what museum patron wants to be remembered for chairs or a burglar alarm, regardless of how much he loves his museum?) Furthermore, the purchase was a social necessity, since the museum, serving a large audience, had no significant collection of contemporary art, from which local students, citizens, artists, could learn.

We had returned to education, from whence we had started with groups (the museum's primary means of educating its public). We had completed the full circle.

'Our first responsibility is to the object, and to the person who wants to respond to it in a private way,'[1] Sherman Lee, director of the Cleveland Museum has written, expressing a very traditional idea. Although some people might call this elitist, I think that it is eminently valid, especially at present. The museum audience has grown so much in ten years that active proselytism is no longer required to bring the public to art. The public has arrived, and by now the museum audience has also gained considerable experience. Perhaps the museum has not taken full stock of this, for it continues to contrive schemes to attract crowds.

In 1963 the *Mona Lisa* was exhibited in the Metropolitan Museum in New York. It has been described how 'day after day, the line would start to form on the front steps long before the museum opened at ten o'clock. By mid-morning it stretched south for several blocks, inching forward imperceptibly, oblivious to rain, snow, sleet, or the occasional New York combination of all three. Guards maintained the ranks inside the museum, channelling them across the main hall, down the early Christian corridor to the right of the staircase (its walls turned black by the end of the first week), through the next gallery, and into the medieval hall where the *Mona Lisa* hung. The picture was flanked by two guards and watched from behind the choir screen by detectives. Another museum attendant exhorted the pilgrims to keep moving. No one was allowed to pause in front of the shrine, and once past it the anointed were funnelled out through a side entrance into the museum parking lot. . . . Explanatory panels had been posted along the visitors' route, with photographic blowups of the eyes, the mouth, the hands, and the far distant landscape; in his essay for the special *Mona Lisa* catalogue, Theodore Rousseau had urged viewers to try to put out of their mind everything they had ever heard or read about the picture, and to approach it in terms of feeling rather than understanding. How many did so? How many saw only a watery blur labelled "famous painting," and took away . . . no more than the knowledge that they had seen it?'[1]

The exhibition, which drew one million viewers, had some of the overtones of a circus, but also contained the promise of exposing the people to a new kind of experience, an experience which for many would later be deepened. When the *Mona Lisa* travelled abroad again, to Tokyo in 1974, the renewal of the extravaganza, and the controversy caused by the manner in which the painting was displayed, reflected in a symbolic way the inertia that seems to plague art-preserving institutions. If the gesture was mildly outrageous in 1963, in 1974 it is completely obscene.

In opting for crowds, museums have largely forgotten the rights of the individuals who comprise those crowds, and the integrity of the individual object. They have relegated an intimate and uplifting experience to the level of recreation. In fact, exhibition-going is very good entertainment, but the art object also has another, sometimes forgotten, capacity to contribute to the life of the spirit. It is surely this spiritual allotment which is its greatest value; and it is surely this value which, at the cost of all else, should be preserved.

POSTSCRIPT

Theft and pillage, smuggling and speculation, overcrowded museums and inflated prices in the sale room: one or another of these phenomena touches everyone who is interested in art, and each is part of a general malaise which constitutes a real threat to the spiritual enrichment we expect from works of art. This malaise, the result of the current confusion between the material and spiritual value of artworks, can easily be recognized as the force behind the illicit art market and the destruction it causes.

More subtly, the pre-eminence of material evaluations in all we hear about art has also resulted in a certain atrophy of our own values. When we read of an art theft, we cannot help being impressed or shocked in proportion to the financial worth of the works involved; when a great exhibition is mounted, we are made to appreciate the huge cost of assembling and insuring the presentation; when an object is sold, its value, and the buyer's satisfaction, are often measured by the size of the price it brings. The 'importance' of a work of art is linked, even in the art lover's mind, to its capacity to yield a return. One is almost alarmed today by the idea of bargains in art.

A certain toleration for the abuse of art is thus built into the very framework of our consciousness of the art world.

If asked to evaluate the function of art in life, most people would say that art is something which allows us to look up from our own, sometimes petty, preoccupations; a reminder that there are different ways than our own of seeing life. A work of art can provide a sanctuary or a challenge to the spirit, depending on the work and on the individual's needs and moods. In this sense it can be a spiritual relaxant, an important and highly refined form of recreation – what Matisse referred to as 'a soothing, calming influence on the mind, something like a good armchair which provides relaxation from physical fatigue.'

This does not, however, mean that art should be peripheral, excluded from daily life. Ideally, in fact, art would be integral to the rest of one's life, a process which would lend a certain 'art' to life itself, and to every human product. 'Art,' as Thomas Aquinas has written, 'is the principle of Nature in her manner of operation: Art is the principle of manufacture.'

One basic fault in our contemporary aesthetic structure is that we have come to isolate art from life as something totally useless. The idea that art serves no useful function has come to serve as a symbol for its purity. This is a natural enough association, for it is an attempt to see the purity of art as untainted by commerce, untouched by mammon. But unfortunately, the premise of the uselessness of art has had the opposite effect: when set apart from life, isolated within what is sometimes called the 'masterpiece complex', art becomes so precious that its ultimate value is as its own antithesis: as a commodity, a useful means of commercial exchange.

In an ideal world works of art would be available to whomever desired or had need of them; every person would be able to possess at least one object of a certain quality, and to enjoy other objects as common property, not to look at as precious curiosities, but to use for their capacity to expand and transfigure our thoughts and perceptions. Even in the real world, in fact, art has until recently been able to fulfil this goal more or less satisfactorily, and to dissociate itself from the most distasteful aspects of marketing. Whatever their other motivations may have been, collectors in the past did not hope to make a profit on collecting art, and the desire to own and enjoy art objects was formerly limited to a small part of the population.

Today we could not, even if we wanted to, return to former conditions in which art was not popular enough to draw the attention of speculators and thieves. To restore the balance between the value and function of works of art would require much rethinking and redirecting of cultural policy on the institutional, governmental, and even international level. For the present, therefore, it might be well to think of some constructive actions in which all of us might engage to reduce the present crisis.

The crisis in art is a complex mixture of many distressing phenomena. Some, like the looting of local antiquities, will have to be controlled by the governments of the countries involved, seeking solutions to the problem which satisfy all the interested parties; others, like art theft, will require more organized collaboration on an international level, to prevent stolen art from being negotiable; still others will require an overhaul of the ethics of the art trade.

Yet there are some aspects of the problem which the public can help to change, often through simple actions directed at the most mundane aspects of the art crisis – those which, in truth, most affect our lives. For example: the art owner who has photographs of all the objects in his possession is helping, in the event of theft, to combat the illicit market, which depends on the fact that most stolen art cannot be identified. The tourist who refuses to buy antiquities in a country where their export is forbidden is exercising a boycott against a system which commits important abuses. A museum visitor who complains about viewing conditions, points out the vulnerability to theft or vandalism of a certain object, or otherwise makes his voice heard, can influence the ideas of the museum staff about what its public wants.

More important, perhaps, is the influence that the public can exert on the overall climate of the art market. Increased public consciousness of the situation has already led to many changes, and it is here that our greatest hope seems to lie. In the last few years the simple influence of public outrage has had much to do with the outcome of such controversies as those over museum entry fees, museums returning smuggled art, and 'de-accessioning'. The art consumer (would it be absurd to suggest the formation of Art Consumers' Associations?) should continue to make his viewpoint known by expressing his outrage at the abuses of art which he is commonly required to tolerate. More profoundly, each 'art consumer' should perhaps reconsider his own idea of what art should be – and to what degree he endorses the idea that the value of an art object is 'what somebody will pay for it.'

The central question of the art crisis is whether the inflation of art prices, which provides the fuel for the other workings of the system, will continue as it has. If it does, the present crisis can only be expected to worsen. To prevent this, the consumers of art – including museums, collectors, and modest individual buyers – would have to work together voluntarily to limit the level to which art prices can climb. Such an effort would, of course, involve a certain amount of austerity, and a change in our principles of consumption. To a certain extent, such a change is already beginning to take place. The publicity the antiquities crisis has received has given many countries the impetus to update their methods of dealing with this problem; the alarming competition for masterpieces has led museums to consider exchange, rather than acquisition, as a means of broadening their scope.

We can only hope that this kind of action will become more and more common, turning the direction of events before the objects still available are totally depleted, or placed under lock and key. In such an effort, individual consciousness of the problem and its consequences could lead to increased public pressure on the institutions that can affect change. The action stimulated by public concern could be the deciding element in ameliorating a crisis before it becomes an irreversible disaster.

NOTES

p. 88, 1. Douglas Barrett, *Early Chola Bronzes*, Bombay, 1965, p. 32.
p. 103, 1. Cornelius Vermeule, quoted in Robert Taylor, 'Gods, Graves and Smugglers,' *Boston Sunday Globe*, 12 April 1970, p. 16.
p. 105, 1. 'Lydia' in *Metropolitan Museum of Art Bulletin*, XXVI, 5, January 1968, p. 197.
p. 106, 1. George M. A. Hanfmann and A. H. Detweiler, 'Sardis though the Ages,' *Archaeology*, XIX, 1, April 1966, p. 94.
p. 106, 2. George M. A. Hanfmann, 'Sardis Excavations, 1961,' *Archaeology*, XV, 1, March 1962, p. 60.
p. 106, 3. George M. A. Hanfmann, 'Sardis 1966,' *Archaeology*, XX, 1, January 1967, p. 66.
p. 107, 1. Robert Taylor, 'Gods, Graves and Smugglers,' *Boston Sunday Globe*, 12 April 1970.
p. 113, 1. Dwight B. Heath, 'Economic Aspects of Commercial Archaeology in Costa Rica,' *American Antiquity*, XXXVIII, 3, July 1973, p. 263.
p. 113, 2. *ibid.* p. 264.
p. 115, 1. Dwight B. Heath, 'In Quest of "El Dorado": Some Sociological Aspects of Huaquerismo (Pot-Hunting) in Costa Rica,' *Anales del Instituto de Geografia e Historia de Costa Rica, 1967-68, 1968-69*, San José, Costa Rica, 1971.
p. 115, 2. Report presented to International Council of Museums published in *Icom News*, XXV, 3, September 1972, p. 181.
p. 132, 1. 'African Wares Trek to the Art Market,' *Business Week*, 15 July 1972, p. 91.

p. 134, 1. J. A. R. Wembah-Rashid, 'Isinyago and Midimu, Masked Dancers of Tanzania and Mozambique,' *African Arts*, IV, 2, Winter 1971, p. 43.

p. 137, 1. Thomas Hoving quoted in Barbara Goldsmith, 'The True Confessions of Thomas Hoving,' *New York*, 16 April 1973, p. 72.

p. 137, 2. *ibid.*, p. 73.

p. 137, 3. *ibid*, p. 73.

p. 142, 1. Gladys Weinberg, Letter to *Icom News*, 1970.

p. 143, 1. Allen Wardwell, 'Mayan Treasures at the Art Institute of Chicago,' *Apollo*, XCV, no. 124, June 1972, p. 491–2.

p. 143, 2. Clemency Coggins, 'Archaeology and the Art Market,' *Science*, CLXXV, 4019, January 1972, p. 264.

p. 146, 1. Cornelius Vermeule quoted in Peter Hopkirk, 'Smuggled Treasure from Royal Tomb Turns up in Museum,' London *Times*, 31 January 1970.

p. 150, 1. Karen O. Bruhns, 'The Methods of *Guaqueria*: Illicit Tomb Looting in Colombia,' *Archaeology*, XXVI, 3, April 1972, p. 143.

p. 154, 1. From the letter of resignation of Fernando Garavito.

p. 168, 1. Norton Simon in Foreword to *Three Centuries of French Art: Selections from the Norton Simon, Inc. Museum of Art and The Norton Simon Foundation*, 1973.

p. 168, 2. David L. Shirey, 'Norton Simon Bought Smuggled Idol,' *New York Times*, 12 May 1973.

p. 170, 1. William McCleery, 'A Businessman and Art Collector Talks of Art (and Business),' *University*, no. 60, Spring 1974, p. 13.

p. 170, 2. Norton Simon is a regent of the University of California and a trustee of Reed College, in Portland, Oregon. He has been chairman of the Carnegie Commission on Future Higher Education, and belongs to the Institute of Advanced Studies at Princeton University. Until he resigned in 1971, he was the most influential trustee of the Los Angeles County museum. He personally, and through Norton Simon Inc., supports six foundations: the Norton Simon Foundation; the Norton Simon Foundation for Education (which awards scholarships); the Norton Simon Inc. Museum of Art;

Foundation Funds of Norton Simon Inc. (California); Foundation Funds of Norton Simon Inc. (New York); and the Fullerton Foundation.

p. 171, 1. McCleery, *op. cit.*, p. 10.

p. 172, 1. David L. Shirey, 'The Norton Simon Inc. Collection: Distinguished and Eclectic,' *Art News*, LXXI, 12, December 1972, p. 24.

p. 172, 2. Steven V. Roberts, 'Why a 63-Year-Old Tycoon Worth $100 Million Wants to Run for the Senate', *New York Times Magazine*, 31 May 1970.

p. 174, 1. Alice B. Saarinen, *The Proud Possessors*, New York, 1958, p. 373.

p. 175, 1. Mahonri Sharp Young, 'Letter from U.S.A.; Rembrandt Heeramaneck, and Dine,' *Apollo*, LXXXV, no. 60, February 1967, p. 143.

p. 175, 2. Nasli Heeramaneck in Foreword to *The Arts of India and Nepal: the Nasli Heeramaneck Collection*. Boston Museum of Fine Arts, 1966.

p. 176, 1. Grace Morley, 'Museum Collection for India, pre-Columbian Art as New-Note,' *Journal of Indian Museums*, XXI-XXIV, 1965–8, p. 24.

p. 195, 1. Recounted orally to the author by Stanley Clark.

p. 195, 2. From 'Sotheby Anecdotes' distributed by Sotheby's press office.

p. 196, 1. *ibid.*

p. 197, 1. Souren Melikian, 'What the Turnover Figures Really Mean,' *International Herald Tribune*, 11–12 August 1973.

p. 198, 1. *Art at Auction* 1970–71, London, 1971, p. 455.

p. 199, 1. Sotheby's Belgravia, *A Sale of 19th and 20th Century Collectors' Items*, Friday, 18 May 1973, Lot 12.

p. 200, 1. *ibid.*, lot 22.

p. 200, 2. *ibid.*, lot 167.

p. 201, 1. *ibid.*, lot 10.

p. 202, 1. John Russell in Foreword to *Christie's Review of the Year 1968–69*, London, 1969, p. 10.

p. 212, 1. Geraldine Norman, 'Fuss About an Icon Helps to Raise Price by £4340,' London *Times*, 31 October 1973.

p. 226, 1. Julian Agnew, 'Art for Art's Sake – or as an Investment?' *The Daily Telegraph*, 7 July 1973.

p. 232, 1. Roland Redmond quoted in Calvin Tomkins, *Merchants and Masterpieces*, New York, 1973, p. 338.

p. 233, 1. Hedrick Smith, 'Art for Everybody – Too Much of a Good Thing?' *International Herald Tribune*, 2 January 1973.

p. 233, 2. *ibid.*

p. 235, 1. Quoted in Max Kozloff, 'Under the Corporate Wing,' *Art in America*, no. 59, July 1971, p. 98.

p. 238, 1. Sherman Lee quoted in Calvin Tomkins, *op. cit.*, p. 343.

p. 239, 1. *ibid.*, p. 341–2.

INDEX

INDEX